The
Special Educational
Needs Coordinator

Maximising your potential

Vic Shuttleworth

PEARSON EDUCATION LIMITED

Head Office:
Edinburgh Gate
Harlow CM20 2JE
Tel: +44 (0)1279 623623
Fax: +44 (0)1279 431059

London Office:
128 Long Acre
London WC2E 9AN
Tel: +44 (0)20 7447 2000
Fax: +44 (0)20 7240 5771
Website: www.educationminds.com

First published in Great Britain in 2000

© Pearson Education Limited 2000

The right of Vic Shuttleworth to be identified as Author
of this Work has been asserted by him in accordance
with the Copyright, Designs and Patents Act 1988.

ISBN 0 273 65005 X

British Library Cataloguing in Publication Data
A CIP catalogue record for this book can be obtained from the British Library.

10 9 8 7 6 5 4 3 2

Typeset by Boyd Elliott Typesetting.
Printed and bound in Great Britain by Redwood Books Ltd, Trowbridge, Wilts.

The Publishers' policy is to use paper manufactured from sustainable forests.

About the author

VIC SHUTTLEWORTH has been in education for thirty years. Most of his long teaching career was spent in inner-city comprehensive schools. A popular and successful teacher, he headed one of the largest subject departments in the country before moving on to senior management positions in schools and LEAs. Vic Shuttleworth is a very experienced OFSTED inspector and teacher-trainer and has been employed as a management consultant by several schools. He has run successful courses for school managers for the Centre for Research in Teaching, based at Birmingham University, and is a member of the Institute of Management. He has extensive experience of teaching children with learning difficulties and has inspected SEN in many schools. A qualified inspector of special schools, he has worked with both mainstream and special school staff on the development of effective management practice and curriculum innovation. He has also been responsible for an 'English as a Second Language' teaching unit, has advised schools on whole school literacy policies and worked with Chambers of Commerce on the development of basic skills accreditation. He is author of 'Middle Management in Schools'. At present he is a Director of Bench Marque Limited, one of the country's largest and best known inspection and consultancy companies, and heads its Training Division.

'If I have seen further it is by standing on the shoulders of giants.'

Isaac Newton, 1676

Contents

Series editor's introduction

The nature of schools and the educative process is changing. Indications are that the first decade of the twenty-first century will see the fastest, and the most far-reaching, changes in schools and schooling since the compulsory education system was established. The signs are there if we have eyes to see them:

- advances in technology will alter the nature of learning. While school has been characterised by the need for groups of people to assemble together to listen to a teacher, the computer, its software and the Internet are making learning accessible to anyone, according to need and inclination, without their having to come together;

- technology, through the computer and through video-conferencing, gives access on a local level to global opportunities. If they have the technology, pupils in Britain can access the very best lessons and the very best teachers from anywhere in the world. In place of thousands of teachers teaching thousands of different, more or less good, lessons on a topic, the student will be able to access the most complete and dynamic lesson regardless of where it is taught;

- computers even threaten the concept of school time. Since the computer gives access at unlimited times and in unlimited places, learning need no longer be associated with time slots at all;

- but it is not just computers that are driving the forces of education into new channels. Economics plays a part. School buildings are inflexible and costly, yet they often remain unused for more than 80 per cent of the time – during vacations, evenings, nights and so on. Costly plant lying idle is a luxury that society may feel unable to afford;

- increasingly, we can see non-teachers of various kinds becoming more central to the education process. There was a time when no adult but a teacher would have been found in a classroom. Now schools often have a greater complement of technicians, administrators, nursery assistants, special needs assistants, students from care courses, voluntary helpers and counsellors than they do of teaching staff.

So key areas – how learning takes place, where it takes place, when, its quality, the type of plant required, the nature of the people who deliver it – are all in the melting pot as we enter the new millennium. If ever there was a moment for developing a new breed of educational leaders who could span the effective management of the present system and forge a path into the future, this is it.

This series is therefore dedicated to achieving those ends: to help education managers at various levels in the system to become the leaders now and the pioneers of the future. The titles are all written by people with proven track records of innovation. The style is intended to be direct, and the reader is asked to engage with the text in order to maximise the training benefit that the books can deliver.

Change is rarely comfortable, but it can be exciting. This series hopes to communicate to school leaders something of the confidence that is needed to manage change, and something of the fulfilment that comes from meeting challenge successfully.

Professor Trevor Kerry

Glossary

ADHA	–	Attention Deficit Hyperactivity Disorder
ASPERGER'S SYNDROME	–	A mild autistic disorder characterised by awkwardness in social interaction, slow and deliberate speech and preoccupation with very narrow interests (Hans Asperger, Austrian psychiatrist).
AUTISM	–	A mental condition characterised by great difficulty in communicating with others and in using language and abstract concepts.
CA	–	Classroom Assistant
COP	–	Code of Practice
DDP	–	Departmental Development Plan
DfEE	–	Department for Education and Employment
DYSLEXIA	–	A disorder involving difficulty in learning to read or interpret words, letters and other symbols. (ALEXIA gives the same symptoms but is usually the result of brain damage.)
DYSPHASIA	–	A language disorder marked by deficiency in the generation of speech due to brain disease or damage.
DYSPRAXIA	–	A developmental disorder of the brain in childhood causing difficulty in activities requiring coordination and movement. Known also as 'clumsy child syndrome'.
EBD	–	Emotional and Behavioural Difficulties
ED. PSYCH.	–	Educational Psychologist
ESN	–	Educationally Sub-Normal
HMI	–	Her Majesty's Inspector of schools

IBP	–	Individual Behaviour Plan
ICT	–	Information and Communications Technology
IEP	–	Individual Education Plan
ITT	–	Initial Teacher Training
LEA	–	Local Education Authority
LMS	–	Local Management of Schools
LSA	–	Learning Support Assistant
NFER	–	National Foundation for Educational Research
PAP	–	Personal Action Plan
PSP	–	Pastoral Support Plan
SAT	–	Standard Assessment Test
SDP	–	School Development Plan
SEN	–	Special Educational Needs
SENCO	–	Special Educational Needs Coordinator
SI	–	Statutory Instrument
SOW	–	Scheme of Work
SMT	–	Senior Management Team
TQM	–	Total Quality Management

List of tasks

List of tables

List of figures

Acknowledgements

Certain materials are reproduced from OFSTED and DfEE publications. The individual publications are acknowledged in the text or footnotes. These extracts are subject to Crown copyright. Crown copyright is reproduced with the permission of the Controller of Her Majesty's Stationery Office.

Some materials reproduced in the sections on leadership and development planning are taken from programmes for the professional development of teachers written in conjunction with the Centre for Research in Teaching, Newman College, University of Birmingham. Permission has been granted for these materials to be reproduced.

Particular thanks go to the many SENCOs with whom I have worked, and whose schools I have inspected, for showing me the very wide range of approaches to the post. Especial gratitude is reserved for Nancy Pearson, Special Educational Needs Coordinator at Dunchurch Boughton C of E (Aided) Junior School in Warwickshire, who provided me with many valuable insights into the discharge of management responsibilities in the primary sector.

Finally, my most sincere thanks go to my colleague and friend Vi Parfitt whose dedication and skill in word processing the manuscript made this book possible.

Preface

This book has 'management' as its central theme. It is written primarily for new or aspirant postholders who wish to get to grips with the key skills needed for the effective discharge of a range of responsibilities. It is not a book about children who have 'special needs' or how to teach them, although these topics are given proper and relevant attention.

Central to the work of all schools is the process of planning what pupils will learn, teaching appropriate skills and knowledge, and assessing pupils' understanding so that progress is ascertained before the process begins again. Schools plan for a wide range of attitudes and abilities in pupils, and most children learn and progress satisfactorily within the system. Some children, however, progress at a different pace from the majority and these pupils may have special educational needs at both ends of the ability spectrum. Reliable evidence suggests that some 20 per cent of the school population has a special need at some stage, and a smaller percentage experiences difficulty with learning beyond school into adulthood. Nor are special needs confined to those who find aspects of learning difficult. A significant minority of our pupils are exceptionally gifted, either all round or in one particular aspect, and without specialist attention talented children can become easily disaffected or deprived. Teaching children with special needs is the most challenging, frustrating but ultimately one of the most rewarding experiences to be found in education. The work is at the extreme edge of teaching skill and relies more heavily upon our knowledge of the physical and psychological bases of children's learning than any other branch of education.

Following the publication in 1994 of the DfEE's Code of Practice on the identification and assessment of special educational needs a new post was created in schools, that of Special Educational Needs Coordinator, or SENCO. The function of the SENCO is to coordinate the school's policy and provision across the *whole* curriculum and in many schools this onerous job is the only whole school management post outside the Senior Management Team. The post is heavily bureaucratic in nature and many existing SENCOs claim that their job is virtually impossible to carry out effectively.

One reason for this is a decade of continuous and relentless reform in education which has brought the teaching profession under public scrutiny in a manner not experienced by any other sector of society. Schools have been subjected to open analysis of their strengths and deficiencies and have therefore responded in equally transparent ways. The watchword is *'standards'* – how high are the educational standards achieved by the nation's children when measured by test and examination results and are they high enough? What is the capacity of each school to improve and are all schools sufficiently 'professional' in their management outlook to apply that capability? It is easy to see how some children and their teachers feel somehow left behind by all of this, that their efforts are unrecognised and therefore unrewarded so their life expectations diminish.

One response to change has been to create additional posts of responsibility in schools while at the same time allowing other more 'traditional' positions to become less influential or even to have them wither away completely. With openness and transparent accountability in mind schools have adopted the 'best fit' approach, and this is the way it should be. In other words, the person selected to do a job is the best person for that job, not the longest serving or the next in line for promotion. This, of course, creates its own set of problems, both for the school and for new postholders:

- most new positions expect the successful combination of both teaching and management duties;
- there is a higher set of expectations, often measurable and linked to remuneration, of the levels of performance of the postholder;
- the new posts are much more publicly accountable for perceived outcomes in relation to resources committed;
- the management 'ethos' needs to be more 'professional' and linked to clearly delineated responsibilities and training in key skills; and
- there is less emphasis on 'doing' and more on 'persuading others to contribute'.

Moreover, although many schools were quick to seize upon opportunities to create new management structures in the belief that new challenges demanded radical responses, the role descriptions or job specifications did not match the innovative thinking which created them and tended to be couched in traditional administrative or bureaucratic task terms.

The book's key message to newly appointed postholders is that the role of SENCO is not what it was. SENCOs themselves have expanded the role and extended their influence over such matters as curriculum development, teaching styles and professional development to the extent that in many schools the role is pivotal to strategic management. This has largely been achieved by the individuals themselves who have manoeuvred their schools into positions of maximum receptiveness to the challenges which lie ahead.

It is how existing, newly appointed or aspirant SENCOs learn to accept the challenge of this emerging role and are given guidance on acquiring the key management skills which accompany both present responsibility and future authority which is the cornerstone of this book.

How to use this book

This book aims to enable aspiring or newly-appointed SENCOs to approach a range of management tasks with the right knowledge and techniques, to work systematically and effectively with colleagues for the benefit of our most vulnerable children and to cut through the layers of bureaucracy to expose the bigger issues. In short, it is not a guide to working harder, it is a guide to working *smarter*. The book is unique in that its focus is on the very specific management skills needed for effectiveness in one specialised role within schools. Unlike other management positions the post of SENCO is one that *any* teacher, regardless of subject background, can aspire to. This book shows how teachers can make the transition from teaching to management and maximise their potential for combining the roles successfully and effectively.

There is very little material available to schools which guides specific postholders through essential management tasks and enables them to identify and practise new skills. Most published work on Special Needs concentrates on pupils' problems and corrective strategies rather than on the extensive management issues faced by SENCOs. This book concentrates on the practical management skills needed by SENCOs in a variety of realistic contexts. There is a balance between theory and practice and the book may be studied as a complete comprehensive guide or each chapter may be taken as a discrete unit and the range of topics covered applied to the individual needs of the reader. Each chapter contains topic-specific theoretical information illustrated by charts, tables, discussion exercises and case-study examples drawn from research into existing best practice found in actual schools. Chapters also contain checklists and practical guides to identifying and solving common problems, and each chapter has management effectiveness in the SENCO role as its principal theme. Taken as a whole, the book offers a progressive study from the point of obtaining a post in a school to the acquisition of advanced management skills.

The book preaches proactive rather than reactive management as its central tenet and forces prospective or novice SENCOs to think about the essential leadership and management roles implicit in placing the needs of all children at the core of our thinking about the curriculum. Each chapter gradually illustrates the shift away from 'doing' to 'persuading' and stresses the need for high quality expert knowledge applied in an advisory capacity. The nub of a SENCO's responsibility is to effectively manage the school's policy in partnership with others and each chapter illustrates the skills needed for this essentially relationship-based role. The book teaches that to be successful, SENCOs should be good organisers, be assertive without dominance, have the personal credibility to persuade others, be sufficiently flexible in outlook to absorb change and be able to intervene expertly at a number of different levels.

Above all, the book aims to answer the following ten key questions and each chapter either unfolds the answers, or the means of obtaining them becomes clearer:

1 What will be my main responsibilities and to whom am I accountable for their discharge?

2 How has the SENCO role developed since its inception and how can I influence further development?

3 How do I prepare the whole school for the challenges of inclusive education?

4 How can I influence the curriculum and teacher colleagues especially when SEN pupils cannot meet school or national targets?

5 How can I learn, develop and practise new management skills?

6 How do I combine whole school responsibilities with a significant personal teaching commitment?

7 How can I ensure that children make good progress in all curriculum areas?

8 How do I influence the construction of a school policy for SEN which places and maintains SEN at the centre of school life and not on the margin?

9 How do I become an effective team leader?

10 How do I cope with an OFSTED inspection?

These are essentially *management* questions, asked by inexperienced SENCOs, and are nothing to do with the mechanics of teaching except as they relate to the work of colleagues. Keep the questions in mind, note the extent of the answers and see how the book's Tailpiece advises on how they may be taken on to further applications and the acquisition of more advanced management techniques.

Throughout the book there are frequent references to the Code of Practice. Although there is a revision to the Code planned for September 2000, all references are to the 1994 version, the fundamental principles of which will be embodied in the new Code.

The contents, index and glossary pages help the reader to find the best route through the book to satisfy individual requirements, and each chapter refers to sections in other chapters which extend or complement knowledge of the topic under review. Each chapter is also summarised twice to enable the reader to gain an overall topic impression: the start of the chapter outlines the main areas to be covered and at the end of each chapter is a concise bullet point summary of the main skills covered with appropriate action points.

chapter one

Personal attributes and expertise

Introduction

'So you want to be a SENCO?'

A SENCO is a coordinator of provision for pupils with special educational needs in a school. Sounds simple enough, and you would not be reading this if you did not have at least a modicum of interest in the subject! The question is, what sort of a SENCO do you want to be? It is more than just being good at the job, it is a matter of joining the ranks of an army of dedicated professionals who have left the minimalist Code of Practice definition far behind and who are now exercising real influence over the curriculum, for it is to the curriculum that we must look for the roots of all problems. In giving serious consideration to the matter of whether to become a SENCO, aspirant postholders should ask themselves this question and think deeply about the answer:

'Are children with special needs failing in the system or are they being failed by the system?'

The answer to this question will say much about the aspirant SENCO's knowledge and ambitions, but to a degree it all depends upon circumstances and size and type of school. In a small primary school the work of a SENCO may be seen as very much a subordinate 'extra' on top of a full-time teaching commitment to a class. Colleagues have other curriculum responsibilities too, so this is just one more task to add to all the rest. There is no room for a philosophy or style, it is simply a matter of accomplishing routine tasks. In these circumstances a teacher with a reputation for sympathetic teaching of pupils with learning difficulties may be asked to 'take it on' because the school wishes to absorb the Code of Practice and that means having a SENCO. That is one type of SENCO and many schools are well served in this fashion: the system is solid and dependable and the school has clear and laudable values to which all pupils are expected to conform. It is not possible, however, to exist in this 'comfort zone' for long. To be sure, time must be found for the daily administrative routines such as compiling and updating the register but other colleagues have similar problems coordinating literacy or science across all classes. The real problem concerns the acquisition of specialist knowledge so that the specific needs of individual pupils can be accurately diagnosed and the subsequent advice to colleagues correctly identified, with appropriate strategies. This is a heavy burden and there is a measure of personal accountability for the wrong diagnosis and the wrong corrective measures. Newly appointed or aspirant SENCOs should be aware of this shift in expectations on the part of colleagues: 'Don't ask me, I only fill in the forms' is not a satisfactory answer to a hard-pressed colleague desperate to find a way through to a child who disrupts her class but who may be autistic. The forces of 'inclusion' are gathering ominously just over the hill so the prospect of each school housing a very wide and complex range of special needs is very real. SENCOs in the administrative comfort zone will therefore need to plan very seriously for their own professional development. Headteachers too need to realise that the chances of appointing a ready-made 'expert' are remote except in the largest of institutions, so a programme of staff development needs to be part of the appointment 'package'.

A significant extra responsibility also falls on the shoulders of SENCOs in primary schools. All the advice and research point to *early identification* as the key to meeting the special needs of the majority of pupils. Secondary school SENCOs usually have good systems for screening tests and have developed good links with SENCOs in 'feeder' schools, but where does the primary school SENCO turn for 'early' identification of needs? There is a very heavy reliance on nursery and infant colleagues in a situation where special needs in the early years is notoriously difficult to define and sometimes to detect. The awareness of the need to acquire, disseminate and apply expertise is an aspect of each aspirant SENCO's preparation for the role.

At the opposite end of the spectrum of SENCO 'types' is the Head of Learning Support in a large secondary school with above average numbers of pupils on the register of special needs and possibly a designated unit on site. Such a person is likely to occupy a position of status and influence which is reflected in teaching commitment, salary and available time for management issues. These 'advantages' are offset by the challenge of compartmentalising the curriculum into academically based, examination results-orientated separate subjects taught by groups of specialists with their own philosophies and agendas. The emphasis in these circumstances is on how the aspirant SENCO perceives his/her ability to manage change, especially attitudinal change. The chief characteristics of this type of SENCO are likely to be professional qualifications in SEN, a long apprenticeship in a learning support environment, a specific professional skill in teaching a particular category of need and the ability to manage a team of colleagues whose sole responsibility is for teaching pupils with special educational needs. Aiming for this kind of position usually involves strong competition from others and the demonstration of a track record acquired elsewhere.

Given the range of schools and circumstances in which SENCOs find themselves it is not possible for this chapter, or indeed this whole book, to deal specifically with the needs of each individual as he or she aspires to the role. However, it is important to consider the role in the context of how it was originally envisaged and to exemplify how it has developed. Teachers who wish to become SENCOs can judge for themselves what *kind* of SENCOs they will work towards becoming.

Role of the SENCO

Throughout the current Code of Practice (Code of Practice on the Identification and Assessment of SEN, 1994) and embedded within the revised version due to come into operation in September 2000 is frequent reference to specific responsibilities which the school, largely through its coordinator for special needs, must discharge. Specifically, the SENCO is responsible for:

■ advising on the content and detail of the school's SEN policy;

■ the day-to-day operation of the policy;

■ liaising with and advising fellow teachers;

■ coordinating provision across the curriculum;

■ compiling and maintaining the SEN register;

■ overseeing and updating all records on pupils with SEN;

■ creating and maintaining communication and consultation with parents;

■ determining and contributing to staff professional development;

■ working in partnership with all external agencies;

■ monitoring and evaluating the effectiveness of policy and procedure.

These responsibilities are examined in further detail in Chapter 5: 'Methodology', but for now it is important for prospective or newly appointed SENCOs to be aware of this list of formal responsibilities and how it may be interpreted in different schools.

Within this list is an indication that the role is wider than the mere teaching of pupils with SEN and even in its original concept we can see the scope for development. For example, experienced SENCOs will say that one of the most significant differences between their role now and what it was a few years ago is that they spend more time advising others on how to do the things that they themselves used to be expected to do. The *advisory* role is now more significant and places greater demands on the SENCO's knowledge and ability to communicate it to colleagues.

The way the role of the SENCO has emerged and is developing is perhaps best seen in relation to the curriculum, and we return now to the question posed earlier as to whether children with special needs are failing in the system or being failed by it. The 'system' is the curriculum. The prevailing view has been that a 'special need' must be defined in relation to a 'norm' and that the norm is the way eighty per cent of the school population reacts to the taught curriculum. The taught curriculum is the fixed reference point and the children are the variables. Furthermore, the curriculum as presented by the National Curriculum is loaded in favour of the 'academic' rather than the aesthetic, creative or practical. Specific skills in literacy and numeracy are needed to unlock areas of the academic curriculum which are not necessarily needed to gain meaningful access to others. It is not surprising, therefore, that special educational needs is defined as an inability to cope with aspects of the curriculum in the same way as the majority of pupils. This is what class and subject teachers witness daily, so their perception of special needs is a child who is finding it difficult to learn a specific skill in relation to a subject. The curriculum is built upon an assumption of mastery of that skill. An inability to learn a skill is not the same as an inability to learn, yet 'provision' and 'support' are nearly always concentrated on corrective strategies limited to a very narrow range of skills. In other words, the child is failing in the curriculum and must be helped to succeed in the curriculum. The most powerful lobby for this view is the need to master the essential skills of reading, and it is difficult to argue convincingly against this, but can the same be said for calculating electrical resistance or finding the area of a triangle?

The significant development in SENCO thinking is to challenge this definition of special educational needs and focus on children as the fixed reference point, thus making the curriculum the variable. In a sense this completes the evolution of philosophy about SEN from *segregation* to *inclusion* via *integration*. The advisory role therefore takes on a new dimension: advising subject and class teachers on how the curriculum can be adapted to fit the child rather than on how the child can be equipped to fit the curriculum. This is the first principle of inclusion and a major challenge for schools.

There are two types of teachers: *discoverers* and *settlers* and both are mutually dependent. Most SENCOs are happy to be 'settlers' operating within a well-defined system and with clear expectations of their role enshrined in a job description linked to the Code of Practice. These SENCOs espouse the virtues of integration by minimising withdrawal and leaning heavily on systems for classroom support. Some SENCOs are 'discoverers' and are exercising a new-found influence over curriculum development by bearing down on subject or class teachers in a concentration of in-service training with the support of senior management. These SENCOs are the champions of inclusion and focus on their role in relation to the whole school rather than to the individual pupil. The 'ideal' SENCO probably lies somewhere between the two.

TASK 1
What kind of SENCO do you wish to be?

What is your answer to the question about the curriculum on page 2?

What is the expectation of the role of the SENCO in your present school?

If you are applying for a SENCO job elsewhere, what do you infer about expectations from the job description?

Are you a 'discoverer' or a 'settler' by nature?

How much of your school's SEN policy is based on the assumption that the child must be made to fit the curriculum? Would you endorse this view in your role of operating the policy or seek to rewrite the policy?

The purpose of this lengthy introduction to an essentially short chapter is to give prospective SENCOs a flavour of the role and highlight how it is possible to exert considerable influence through involvement in whole school developments. Even in the smallest of primary schools the importance of the advisory role cannot be overstated, whoever occupies that role.

———— Experience and qualifications ————

It is unlikely that any school would appoint a SENCO who was not an experienced teacher. This means at least five years' classroom teaching, preferably more. The majority of SENCOs in schools are very experienced long-serving teachers who have acquired the skills and patience necessary to forge meaningful links with some 'difficult' pupils and who have earned the respect of colleagues. Experience is not just related to classroom teaching, it must also be seen in relation to knowledge of how schools work: the management structures, the policy making processes and the involvement in procedures for curriculum and staff development.

The education sector is generally very poor at preparing its people for the next stage of a career, although some schools have a deserved reputation for this. Prospective SENCOs will find it difficult to short-circuit 'experience' but it is important to acquire some essential background by:

- finding out as much as possible about what SENCOs do in other schools;
- volunteering to teach 'bottom' sets or to give classroom support;
- being part of departmental or subject SEN 'link teacher' programmes;
- contributing to any opportunities for policy formulation;
- taking the lead in any 'in house' staff training events.

Above all, it is essential to demonstrate in daily classroom teaching that there is an awareness of the needs of all pupils through planning for differentiated tasks, resources and personal intervention. The skill of a successful teacher of pupils with SEN lies in the amount and pace of progress pupils make, so prospective SENCOs need a solid reputation for this. This means acquiring knowledge and expertise in resources, teaching methods and assessment techniques which have applications in more than one curriculum area.

TASK 2

Evaluating your experience

List the experiences which make you the ideal candidate for a SENCO post.

List the experiences which you have not yet had, the lack of which would impede your application for a SENCO post.

With your headteacher draw up an action plan which is designed to bridge any 'gaps' in your experience.

There are no formal qualifications for becoming a SENCO other than those necessary to become a fully qualified teacher. Since 1997 it has been compulsory for Initial Teacher Training (ITT) to include elements on teaching and supporting children with special educational needs and many colleges or university departments had 'optional modules' in SEN before that, but these tended to be very general and superficial.

Post graduate research, masters or second degree qualifications are a different matter and most colleges and universities offer suitable courses connected with special needs in education. The most popular is the Bachelor of Philosophy in Special Needs Education (B.Phil.) which can be taken by practising teachers through part-time attendance at college or through the Open University. Whilst not an essential qualification this is certainly useful for prospective SENCOs attempting a post in a large secondary school. Similarly, many part-time Masters of Education (M.Ed.) courses have optional specialisms in special needs education and these are worth considering once a SENCO has been in post for a year or so.

Most SENCOs, however, survive quite well on a diet of courses supported by Local Education Authorities (LEAs) and specialist institutes. It is particularly recommended that prospective SENCOs negotiate with the school's staff development coordinator or headteacher to gain a place on:

- a course on diagnostic testing techniques;

- a behaviour management course;

- a Dyslexia Institute course;

- a course on autism, dyspraxia and Asperger's syndrome;

- a course on sign language for teaching deaf children.

These are the most common problems for which expertise is needed and for which advice can be sought.

Finally, it is always worth talking to the Local Education Authority's advisor for special educational needs. He/she can be a valuable source of help and advice and could provide access, for example, to the National Association for Special Educational Needs (NASEN) whose regular publications are an excellent source of information and guidance.

TASK 3

Qualifications and courses

Find out about the qualifications and training obtained by learning support assistants at your school.

Gather as much information as you can about courses and qualifications available locally.

Demonstrate the seriousness of your intentions by enrolling on a course.

———— Personality and aptitude ————

Many schools are using more sophisticated methods for selecting staff, especially where posts carry some form of managerial responsibility. Prospective SENCOs should be aware of the possibility of aptitude profiles and psychometric tests being used during an interview. Categorising the ideal personality for the position of SENCO is rather like asking how long is a piece of string, but experienced postholders can usually list the qualities which are most often put to the test. One such experienced SENCO is Helen.

CASE STUDY

'Helen'

Helen is a special needs coordinator in a junior school with a higher than average proportion of children on the special needs register and a higher than average number of statemented pupils for the size of school. The greater than average proportions reflect the local reputation of the school for its provision for pupils with SEN. Helen has a good reputation with the LEA for the quality of her work and she is often contacted by other local SENCOs for help and advice, mostly about procedural matters. Helen is a full-time class teacher and has arranged for supply cover one afternoon each week to enable her to concentrate on SENCO business. She keeps her skills updated through regular attendance on LEA courses, the most recent being on such topics as EBD (emotional and behavioural difficulties), IEPs (Individual Education Plans), target setting and the Literacy Hour related to children with statements. Helen gives much of her time to advising other teachers but admits to not having much influence over curriculum or assessment matters. In essence, she is a typical highly regarded and very experienced junior school SENCO. Here are her essential personal attributes for an aspiring SENCO:

- good working knowledge of the Code of Practice;
- a 'go-getter' for acquiring extra resources;
- blunt speaking to colleagues, parents and LEA;
- being persistent in the face of obduracy and refusal;
- ability to form good relationships with colleagues and outside agencies;
- ability to establish relationships with children and parents based on trust and respect;
- being well organised and on top of routine paperwork;

- ability to absorb procedural details quickly;

- ability to complete tasks 'in one go';

- experienced in behaviour strategies;

- being fair, adaptable and consistent.

In addition to these attributes, the essential teaching qualities of care, patience and self-sacrifice are obvious requirements. Also, schools are keen to display their values to the world and so frequently require new postholders to share the overarching philosophy and be able to demonstrate this through examples of personal conviction.

Finally, given the importance of the emerging role of SENCOs as powerful agents of curriculum change, the most important personal quality to cultivate is *credibility*. Awareness of status contributes to credibility but only in as much as headteachers allow. Where SENCOs are given low status in the school hierarchy credibility will be at the procedural level. An elevated status indicates that the role is seen to be pivotal to curriculum and staff development so the postholder needs to develop a depth of knowledge and cultivate the ability to persuade colleagues in ways which do not threaten or challenge their professional competence.

TASK 4

Personal qualities

List the personal qualities you think are essential for the 'ideal' SENCO.

Which of these qualities do you already possess and which do you need to cultivate?

———— Becoming a SENCO ————

Having analysed the gaps in knowledge, experience and personal qualities, and having decided what type of SENCO to become, it is now time to either accept the offer or apply for the vacancy. Follow these principles.

- In application forms and on CVs highlight the teaching experiences and professional development which best fit the job on offer; general applications do not usually succeed.

■ Use your accompanying letter to stress your experiences and personal philosophies which match the requirements of the job *in that school*; again, general statements do not warrant shortlisting.

■ Refer to courses attended recently and successes in personal teaching to demonstrate your up-to-date knowledge.

■ Current work in teaching or learning support is vital.

■ A period 'shadowing' a SENCO is useful if it can be arranged. A school which is serious about career development will always make shadowing a viable opportunity for ambitious teachers and headteachers' commitment to staff development can be put to the test over this issue.

■ Study the Code of Practice thoroughly.

■ Interview preparation should be thorough and based on Task 5 which follows.

TASK 5

Preparing for interview

If you are called for interview, prepare answers to the following questions.

■ What do you understand to be the responsibilities of a SENCO as outlined in the Code of Practice?

■ What personal experience, knowledge and attributes do you bring to this post?

■ How would you set about advising colleagues on specific SEN matters such as teaching methods?

■ You have two learning support and four classroom assistants, how would you deploy them and what do you expect their duties to be?

■ You have a duty to implement the school's SEN policy. What will you do if you disagree with aspects of the policy?

■ Two pupils arrive at the school with statements. Both are displaying aspects of special needs which you have not experienced before. How do you proceed?

■ What procedures will you set up to ensure pupils' needs are correctly identified?

■ How do you propose to influence curriculum and staff development?

──────── Summary ────────

- You would not be studying this book if you did not have the serious intention of becoming a SENCO. The question is what type of SENCO do you wish to become? A settler or a discoverer?

- It is necessary to form a view as to whether children are failing in the curriculum or because of it, as this determines the prevailing personal philosophy of each SENCO.

- The SENCO role is developing beyond the Code of Practice definition into areas of real influence over curriculum and professional development.

- Prospective SENCOs should prepare for their future role by examining their qualifications, experience and personal attributes. Table 1.1, which follows, enables aspirant SENCOs to check the progress of their preparation for the role. Addressing any 'gaps' should become part of the personal action plan at the end of Chapter 2. Table 1.1 concludes this chapter.

TABLE 1.1   Preparing to be a SENCO

Use the following items as a checklist. Highlight areas for development.

	Yes	No
Attitude towards relationship between child and curriculum clear		
Decision made between whether to be a discoverer or a settler		
Distinction between advocate of integration or inclusion clear		
Comfortable with advisory role in respect of teaching methods		
Understand advisory role in respect of curriculum adaptation		
Secure in knowledge of Code of Practice		
Staff development role clear		
Necessary experiences all in place		
Personal qualifications and staff development courses in place		
Personal attributes noted and securely in place		
Track record of teaching shows good progress of SEN pupils		
No problem with establishing personal credibility		
Able to dispense advice without threatening professionalism of colleagues		
Good knowledge of how school management works		
Able to manage a team of colleagues		
Specialist knowledge secure		
Code of Practice procedures familiar		
Applications tailored to fit the job		
Interview preparation complete		

chapter two

Following appointment

Introduction

Congratulations! You have just been appointed to the role of SENCO. *Coordinator* defines the nature of what you will be doing from now on. What does that mean? This chapter looks at those first essential steps the new SENCO needs to take upon assuming the post. Although the nature of relationships will be different depending upon whether the post is in a new or existing school, the basic management principles which must be adopted remain the same. This chapter assumes that the new postholder has all the qualities described in Chapter 1, and prepares the way for the management techniques described in Chapters 5 and 6. At the end of the chapter there is a personal action plan. This is also referred to from time to time in other chapters. The purpose of the personal action plan is to enable the newly appointed or aspirant SENCO to identify areas for development, both personal and relating to the school, and to begin to plan the best way to tackle these issues.

The main theme of the chapter is adopting a systematic approach to management so as to leave adequate time for the most important aspect of any middle management post in a school – *teaching*. In addition, the chapter takes the view that the SENCO role is evolving beyond what was originally envisaged by the Code of Practice into areas of profound influence over, for example, curriculum development.

Finally, this chapter is short because many of the areas it covers are more fully explored and developed elsewhere in later chapters.

The SENCO role defined

The idea of someone being responsible for special educational needs is not new of course, and the SENCO role has existed in all but name for many years. Many schools, particularly large secondary schools, have had very successful 'Learning Support' departments (formerly 'Remedial departments') for years, led by very experienced and highly respected teachers. In smaller primary schools expertise has tended to be more scattered amongst most class teachers, with responsibility for adaptations to the curriculum being in the hands of subject coordinators, though even in the smallest of schools one teacher could usually be relied upon as the expert in, say, corrective reading strategies.

The fact that the role existed in some form before the Code of Practice gave it a new name and re-defined its functions is important. The recommendations of the Code were not merely plucked out of the air, they were based on the *existing* best practice seen in many schools and the Code must be seen in the light of an attempt to replicate this best practice in all schools by creating a coherent system. However, the *principal function* of the SENCO's antecedents was more concerned with teaching and less with administration or aspects of management. Small groups of pupils could be put into special classes, often following an entirely different curriculum from other pupils, and the main function of the 'expert' was to teach these groups and occasionally support other teachers. As pupils approached the end of compulsory schooling many simply disappeared from the system at the age of 15, leaving society to pick up the pieces again a few years later in what came to be known as 'Adult Literacy classes'.

The evolution of the SENCO role into the one being defined here is due only in part to the Code of Practice and new SENCOs need a thorough understanding of why the role has developed because this influences the relationships with other colleagues and, especially, the senior management of the school. This also helps when establishing relationships with more experienced SENCOs elsewhere.

TASK 6

Influences on the development of the SENCO role

With colleagues, discuss the impact of the following developments on special educational needs provision in schools. What management skills have become necessary as a result of these developments?

- the raising of the school leaving age to 16;
- GCSE and vocational qualifications;
- the National Curriculum and end of key stage assessments;
- school performance 'league tables';
- teacher appraisal;
- baseline assessment for Reception children;

- the abolition of corporal punishment;
- schools being responsible for budgets (LMS);
- target setting.

It is for individual schools to decide how the SENCO role is to be discharged. At one end of the possible spectrum of circumstances is the headteacher who takes on aspects of the job; at the other a large learning support department with specialists for different areas of responsibility. This chapter assumes that one person of middle management status has been appointed to the job. The 1994 Code of Practice defines the role thus:

> 'In all mainstream schools a designated teacher should be responsible for:
>
> - *the day-to-day operation of the school's SEN policy*
> - *liaising with and advising fellow teachers*
> - *co-ordinating provision for children with special educational needs*
> - *maintaining the school's SEN register and overseeing the records on all pupils with SEN*
> - *liaising with parents of children with SEN*
> - *contributing to the in-service training of staff*
> - *liaising with external agencies including the educational psychology service and other support agencies, medical and social services and voluntary bodies'.*

This list represents the essential *minimum* functions of the SENCO role if the school is to fulfil its obligation to 'have regard to' the Code of Practice. Each statement appears somewhat stark by comparison to the realities of the job, and in 'intelligent schools' the list should be amplified to produce a realistic and workable *job description*.

TASK 7

Creating a job description from the Code of Practice list

Compare the Code of Practice list to your own job description. What has been omitted or added? Which items impose limitations and which are open ended? Re-write your job description at the end of your first term as a SENCO.

We shall return to the Code of Practice list in Chapter 5: 'Methodology' and explore the range of tasks associated with each aspect of the role. In the meantime, in the period immediately after taking up the appointment SENCOs need to review what has already been taking place in the school in order to gain a fuller understanding of the school's own unique approach so far. This needs to be done systematically if valuable time is not to be wasted, and as much as possible needs to be written down. It is a good idea to prepare a list of questions against each item in the Code of Practice list (or job description) and to indicate the possible source of the information. For example, it may be that the headteacher is the most likely source of most information and you need to make the most of limited time by having *one* conversation about several topics rather than several piecemeal conversations at inconvenient times.

TASK 8

Assessing what the school has done previously

Take each item from the Code of Practice list and note:

- where information is located;
- which other colleagues are involved;
- key names and contact details for external agencies;
- areas covered in INSET sessions.

Find out about the programme of meetings where SEN input is expected.

Carefully audit the SEN register to ascertain the progress of the system, e.g. are IEPs used? Stage 4 progress?

Select two or three pupils at random who are at Stages 2 and 3. Arrange to talk to those pupils about their learning problems and their opinions about their lessons and progress. Talk to their teachers about the level of support and guidance they have received to date.

Arrange a meeting with the SEN governor(s) to ascertain level of knowledge and involvement.

As soon as possible after taking up appointment, arrange an informal interim review of pupils with statements.

_____ The SENCO's management responsibilities _____

Later chapters will look in more detail at the _key management_ functions likely to be part of the new SENCO's role, but it is important to establish what those functions may be. Schools take different views on the role of middle managers in broad areas of whole school management, but most schools expect significant contributions, especially where layers of senior management have been taken out of the system. Moreover, the relationship between the SENCO and senior management is crucial if the SENCO's role is to be truly effective in providing pupils with SEN with the greatest possible range of opportunities to make good progress. A later section of this chapter is devoted to this very topic.

In the immediate aftermath of taking up an appointment SENCOs need to clarify expectations. This short case study illustrates the point.

CASE STUDY

Clarifying expectations – 'Max'

Max took up the post of SENCO in a middle school for pupils aged 9–13 at the beginning of the Spring term. His predecessor had retired at the end of the previous Summer term after a period of ill-health which had necessitated lengthy absences from school. The SENCO work had been neglected and very little had been done during the Autumn term, except by the coordinators for English and mathematics. Max had begun his career as a class teacher in a primary school and had spent the previous four years in the Learning Support department of a large local comprehensive school. He had also studied for a part-time B.Phil. in special needs. He was energetic, ambitious and eager to tackle the unsatisfactory state of affairs he found. By the end of his first half-term in post, Max had:

- re-written the school SEN policy;

- moved pupils into different teaching groups;

- introduced a new style of IEP;

- removed the Stage 1 pupils from the register;

- issued a five page document on differentiation to all teachers;

- dominated a coordinators' meeting by highlighting subject areas where pupils were making poor progress;

- written a mini development plan for the remainder of the year outlining the immediate resources needs of each subject area;

- changed the deployment of the four classroom assistants.

All these actions were necessary and, on the face of it, sensible. Unfortunately, Max had not checked the limits of his authority and had not discussed with the headteacher what was expected of him during his first term. Instead of concentrating on the needs of the pupils he had made a number of key management decisions with minimal consultation and had succeeded in upsetting colleagues upon whom reliance was vital. Even though a revised policy was needed he did not have the authority from the governors to write a new one; there was no established 'culture' for the use of IEPs; the 'social mix' of some teaching groups was upset; and subject coordinators resented what they perceived as interference in their subjects.

Given that everything Max did was really needed to 'kick start' provision for special needs in the school, how would you have gone about making the changes without upsetting colleagues?

P.S. Max is now an advisor for SEN in a neighbouring authority!

SENCOs, then, need to ensure that they are clear about their initial management responsibilities. These can and will expand and develop as time goes by and as the new SENCO establishes levels of trust and professional competence. This section of the chapter concludes with Fig. 2.1 which lists the most common management functions of a SENCO. There may be a few more management tasks which are unique to each school, and these should be added.

FIG. 2.1   The SENCO's management tasks

Membership of key committees
Co-opted SMT membership
Leading staff training
Policy formulation
Policy evaluation
Appointment of staff
Curriculum development
Assessment procedures
Reporting to governors
School development planning
School targets

WHOLE SCHOOL
MANAGEMENT
CONTRIBUTIONS

Oversight of specialist unit

Deployment of specialist staff

Maintaining register and records

Monitoring consistency

Developing and monitoring innovations

Developing materials and teaching strategies

Advising and guiding colleagues

Planning coherent learning programmes

Leading a team

Devising communication systems

Liaising with subject heads

Arranging and chairing meetings   SPECIFIC SEN MANAGEMENT TASKS

Managing external links

Deployment of support staff

Consulting with parents

Updating professional skills

Following statutory and LEA procedures

Purchase and deployment of resources

Negotiating and setting targets

Analysing and acting upon assessment data

Arranging testing procedures

Appraisal and motivation of colleagues

Departmental development planning

Personal teaching credibility

Some headteachers can get away with it, but one of the most fundamental truths to be applied to any management post in a school is that if you can't teach, if you fail to 'do the business in the classroom', it doesn't matter how slick you are at the rest of the job, you will never gain the respect of colleagues, pupils or senior staff. And you will certainly not gain the respect of parents with whom it is essential for SENCOs to work! One of the imperative personal attributes listed in Chapter 1 was the capacity to give professional advice to colleagues in a non-threatening and non-condescending manner. Advice will not be accepted unless there is respect.

The need to establish personal teaching credibility will vary according to circumstances. If the appointment is an internal one there should be no real problem, as classroom skill will have been one of the factors in achieving the position. Even in these circumstances there may be an issue if it is a large secondary school and the appointee's skills are only apparent to a small group of colleagues in a particular subject department. In a primary school the SENCO role may be closely allied to responsibility for another curriculum area and will certainly be accompanied by a substantial class teaching load. If the appointment is external then there is a different sort of problem because the classroom skills honed in one school over a period of time require rapid translation to an entirely fresh situation and new colleagues will be watching the new SENCO like hawks. It is harder for SENCOs to adapt to new teaching environments than for other staff because the chances are that some pupils specifically under the SENCO's wing will have emotional and behavioural difficulties. This is why Chapter 1 recommends in-service training in behaviour management. Every school has its initiation test: 'Let's see how the new SENCO handles 7C last lesson of the day!' Make sure you pass the test.

Clearly the establishment of a good teaching reputation takes time, but it is important in the first few days of an appointment to lay down some ground rules. Of particular importance is to clearly demonstrate examples of good practice which could form the basis of future advice to colleagues.

TASK 9

Following your own advice

Without compromising your own teaching style, approach the first few lessons in your new position as if they were 'text book models' of best practice. In particular, make sure these features are noted:

- good discipline and classroom management;
- thorough preparation of the topic/lesson content;
- high expectations of the quality of pupils' work, constantly reinforced;
- lesson well planned for what pupils are expected to learn and objectives made very clear;
- differentiated methods and resources;
- constant praise and encouragement;

- reference to IEPs and pupils' learning targets;
- inclusion of all pupils in discussions or answering questions;
- pupils being clear about what they are expected to do;
- joint planning with support staff and discussion about actual versus expected progress;
- good variety and pace to activities;
- step-by-step building of knowledge towards lesson objective;
- probing open questions to test understanding and progress;
- careful arrangement of how pupils are grouped/seated;
- at least one pupil-centred activity so individuals can be helped;
- time at the end to go back over the learning points, explain the next steps and, if appropriate, set differentiated homework.

These are the main features of all good lessons. Add three more which are specifically good practice in teaching pupils with special needs, including gifted and talented pupils.

-
-
-

There are no secrets to establishing personal teaching credibility, but it must be done. Knowing that it must be done and approaching it methodically is half the battle. The other half is self confidence and a sense of humour. Remember, no matter what else needs to be done and however urgently the systems need putting in place, the *first* priority is to get the teaching right and the principles are the same whether it is a whole class, a small withdrawal group or a one to one. A final tip provided by an experienced SENCO: pupils with special needs seem to spend their whole lives filling out worksheets, surprise them for once by not using any yourself!

Influencing SMT expectations

The relationship between middle and senior managers is critical to the success of any school. There is a far greater sense of partnership in today's schools and many headteachers have worked hard to develop and encourage 'flatter' management structures where there is more sharing of responsibility for whole school issues.

Circumstances vary considerably and it is theoretically easier to inculcate a sense of teamwork in a small primary school with a teaching head than it is in a huge comprehensive school with a status conscious senior management team with salary differentials to match.

However, the relationship between the SENCO and the senior management team, particularly the headteacher, is different, and therefore more critical. The most telling aspect of this is that while it is common for headteachers in smaller schools to take on the role of SENCO, it is less common for them to be the science or literacy coordinator. There is therefore an inbuilt expectation that there are aspects of the SENCO's and headteacher's roles which are compatible and, at times, inseparable. The effective management structure for special educational needs places the SENCO at the centre of a partnership. It is the partnership which determines and delivers the policy; the SENCO holds the partnership together. Fig. 2.2 illustrates this relationship.

FIG. 2.2 The management partnership

It is essential that the new SENCO establishes the ground rules as early as possible and three aspects are important:

- *the communication system* – how information and opinion are normally transmitted in the school. The SENCO needs to work closely with the headteacher on a number of issues so are the normal channels adequate? Does a new system need setting up? Is there a need for a regular scheduled meeting? Is it possible to design a simple proforma for regular updates which guarantees that those updates are given?

- *the parameters of power* – the extent to which the SENCO has the *authority* to take decisions and influence the work of others whose status may be more senior. This is the central dilemma of delegation. *Delegation* is a tiered management tool which senior managers often fail to use to best effect. SENCOs need to establish what sort of delegation applies to them and in what circumstances. The three types of delegation are *task, responsibility, authority*. (There is a fourth type: 'reverse delegation', characterised by such statements as "That's OK, I'll do that", usually followed by "Are you sure?" which means "That's a relief!") The first is very common, the second is becoming more common with enlightened participative management structures, the third is very rare. SENCOs, like other middle managers in schools (and indeed in business and industry) find that one of the most frustrating aspects of the job is to be given responsibility without authority. SENCOs need to establish first whether they have authority and second where it begins and ends. Above all, because we are talking about decisions which may affect the daily working practices of all teachers across the curriculum, it is essential for SENCOs to establish a relationship with the headteacher which is based on mutual trust and confidence so that decisions, especially those involving change or monitoring, are taken with the full authority of the headteacher behind them.

■ *direct involvement* – the extent to which the headteacher and senior staff are participants in the total management of SEN. This is of critical importance for two reasons. First, it is now widely acknowledged that effective leadership and management at both governor and senior management level have a positive impact on provision for SEN. Second, there are aspects of the Code of Practice and other statutory requirements which can *only* be carried out by the headteacher – disapplications from the National Curriculum and referrals for statutory assessment at Stage 4 being the obvious examples. It is important therefore that SENCOs and headteachers establish the procedures by which direct involvement will occur.

For much of the time the kernel of the relationship between the SENCO and headteacher is based on expectations. SENCOs *expect* that their professional judgement will be upheld and endorsed, headteachers *expect* high quality knowledge and expertise to provide them with the advice they need when fulfilling statutory obligations. However, this has to manifest itself in rather more than "I'll fill out the forms and you sign them" syndrome. For senior management to be an effective partner there must be *understanding*. SENCOs must view the first few weeks after taking up the appointment as an opportunity to assess the level of senior management's understanding and to set about improving it. This is largely a question of deciding between an active or passive strategy. The burden of administrative tasks becomes worse if the SENCO waits to be asked. Someone else then controls the agenda and the deadlines. The active approach is best because then the SENCO is more in control of his/her limited time.

TASK 10

Being proactive

Establish with the headteacher the kind of information he/she may want from you and when.

Lay down timescales, for example, say that you will always need three days to put together referral documents.

Be firm about your needs, for example, say that you cannot monitor effectively without occasional supply cover or the head taking your class for an afternoon.

Be clear about the calendar of key dates, for example governors' meetings or deadlines for the annual report.

Negotiate 'protected' non-contact time.

Identify areas for change, improvement or development which only senior managers can deal with.

The 'whole child – whole curriculum' proactive management approach is fully covered in the Tailpiece at the end of this book but there are implications for the SENCO's expectations of the level of understanding and subsequent involvement of senior managers. Headteachers need convincing, through hard evidence, of an often unpalatable truth: children with special educational needs are not necessarily failing *in* the system, they are often being failed *by* the system. Strangely, more people are prepared to concede this point in relation to gifted and talented pupils than for those experiencing difficulties with learning. It is important therefore that SENCOs challenge senior management team (SMT) thinking by identifying those aspects of school organisation which seem to make things worse for some pupils.

TASK 11

Pupils' progress and school organisation

Identify a small group of pupils who are finding it difficult to cope with the 'normal' organisation of the school (timetable, class size, pupil groupings, length of lessons, prevailing teaching strategy).

Suggest organisational changes which could be made under the heading 'The following pupils would make much better academic and attitudinal progress if ....'.

Finally, there is a limit to how much can be achieved immediately after taking up the SENCO post – development takes time. It is essential, however, if problems are to be avoided in future, for SENCOs to be clear about their expectations of specific actions the SMT can take both to support their role and to fulfil the wider brief of putting whole school aims into practice. Table 2.1 lists the aspects SENCOs need to start working on.

TABLE 2.1 Senior management contributions

- Valuing and celebrating the achievements of all pupils equally, publicly and frequently.
- Attention to planning –

    teachers' lesson planning;

    subject curriculum planning;

    subject development planning.

- Compatibility of whole school assessment procedures with those for moving pupils up and down the stages.
- Supporting the specific provision identified in statements.
- Integration of pupils with SEN into all aspects of school life.
- Arrangements for managing any special units.
- Assisting with liaison arrangements between SEN, subject and pastoral staff.
- Consistent approaches to marking, homework, target setting and recording achievement.
- Ensuring all statutory requirements are met.
- Monitoring teaching to ensure the policy is consistently followed.
- Including SEN in school development plans.
- Efficient management of specific SEN funding.

Personal action planning

A systematic approach to management works. Doing things in a haphazard fashion only exacerbates the feelings of being overwhelmed by bureaucracy. Immediately after taking up an appointment there will be much that the SENCO has to do to stay on top of teaching commitments, maintain existing practices and develop new ones. It will be necessary to establish priorities and identify other people from whom assistance, support or authority is needed. Simple action planning helps because it places the focus on the main issues and identifies the action needed without the burden of listing possible outcomes. Items can be purely personal, to do with pupils' progress or some administrative responsibility. The plan does not have to be shown to anybody, it is a way of both quantifying and isolating what an individual needs to do.

The action plan which follows is referred to frequently throughout this book so that a full inventory of possible *management* tasks and techniques to try can be built up using information from other chapters. For newly appointed or aspiring SENCOs the process of action planning is a good discipline because it reinforces the need for a systematic and planned approach to the job, or at least to the many facets of the job which are predictable.

The format of the plan here is merely an example. You need to formulate your own headings and agree a definition of short, medium and long term that can be consistently applied. The action plan should be taken to all meetings, especially those with the headteacher.

TABLE 2.2 Personal action plan

PRIORITY FOCUS * Examples	ACTIONS NEEDED		
	SHORT TERM	MEDIUM TERM	LONG TERM
TEACHING * Objectives:			
MAINTAINING CURRENT SYSTEMS * Objectives:			
DEVELOPING NEW SYSTEMS * Objectives:			

———————— Summary ————————

- The newly appointed SENCO will have much to absorb and plenty to do. Adopting a systematic approach to management responsibilities is vital right from the beginning.

- The SENCO role is developing and the new SENCO must be aware of the development opportunities this presents for the individual. Although the role has existed in most schools for some time, the Code of Practice has re-defined it in terms of coordinating provision across the curriculum instead of merely teaching in a narrowly conceived departmental area.

- There are other influences on the development of the SENCO role in addition to the requirements of the Code of Practice. It is important the new SENCOs have a job description that both matches the Code of Practice and reflects the realities of the individual school.

- A first essential step is to assess what the school has done previously in relation to the list of SENCO responsibilities. This should be followed by a careful analysis of expected management responsibilities, especially those concerned with whole school strategic management.

- Establishing credibility in the classroom is vital because it is in this sphere that respect is earned. Without this respect colleagues will not take seriously the advice which is offered and monitoring of provision across the curriculum will be ineffective.

- It is important to view the position of SENCO as one which creates and sustains a partnership with senior management. The relationship with the headteacher is critical if the school is to recognise and act upon organisational weaknesses which may be contributory factors to pupils having SEN. The boundaries of responsibility and authority are important ones to establish.

- Finally, systematic action planning helps to make sense of the many tasks needing to be done and places the focus on the priority given to the most important immediate areas for attention.

———————————————————

chapter three

Theoretical basis

Introduction

There are fewer examples of practical management guidance in this chapter than in others. It is important that SENCOs gain an early appreciation of the theoretical basis to their work because so much time is spent on the bureaucratic response to national and local regulations. Many SENCOs see this as the negative side of their work: time spent on activities which advance administration represents time lost to the very children who need most teaching – whichever end of the ability spectrum they occupy.

Nevertheless it is important to fully comprehend the essential legislation and to appreciate the theoretical background to the Code of Practice. It is important, too, to position the growing influence of the SENCO firmly within the strategic management of the school so that the term 'special needs' is given the widest possible definition. Finally, it is essential that schools have systems which are firmly embedded in the daily practice of all teachers. National initiatives for 'inclusion' may otherwise founder on the frustratingly inconsistent approach of local authorities, and schools, as usual, will be expected to pick up all the pieces.

Recent historical developments

The 1994 Code of Practice on the Identification and Assessment of Special Education Needs (COP) has resulted in a massive increase in the workload of the teacher responsible for special needs in each school. Despite this it has to be seen as one of the most important documents to emerge from almost two decades of continuous educational reform. The fact that there now *is* a teacher responsible is an important testimony to the influence of the Code, because that was not always the case. Nor was it always the case that special needs was seen as an issue for the whole school and the curriculum in particular. To explain the background to the COP we must delve further back into educational history.

The Education Act 1944 had the effect of guaranteeing education provision to all children except the ones deemed to be 'severely subnormal'. 'Slow learners' were viewed differently from other children and their education was determined by the nature of their impairment rather than by any consideration of broad entitlement. The importance of the 1944 Act was the establishment of the principle that the needs of all children should be met within the school system, yet the system set up was a divisive one and there was separate provision for the 'handicapped' just as there was for 'academic', 'technical' and 'vocational' pupils. In 1945 there emerged the notion of 'categorising' degrees of handicap. *The Handicapped Pupils and School Health Regulations* of that year proposed 11 categories, and local authorities could request a school medical officer to provide evidence of a pupil having one of the categories of 'disability of mind or body' through a 'certificate of ascertainment'. Though not actually required by legislation except in cases where a local authority decided to place a pupil in a special school against parental wishes, 'ascertainment' was used widely by local authorities to place children in 'special' schools. The perception was that these schools were the only ones capable of educating children in these categories. Such children were, in a sense, 'hidden away', and there was little or no transfer to mainstream education. Special education was stigmatised by these pieces of legislation and the gulf between 'special' and 'mainstream' schools became impassable. Added to that was the simplistic view of the post-elementary school curriculum with grammar schools representing the full strength brew and each 'layer' underneath experiencing a more diluted version until special schools were reached where the curriculum consisted of simple vocational instruction as a pale imitation of that found in secondary modern schools. But then jobs were cheap and plentiful in the early 1950s!

A little over twenty years after the wartime legislation came the Plowden Report in 1967. Much criticised for its emphasis on how education should be used to overcome the effects of social and economic deprivation, the Plowden committee's report nevertheless had a profound effect on education policy-making right through until the 1980s. Most of today's older generation of teachers were trained in colleges which espoused the Plowden philosophy. In response to special needs the Plowden Report was important in two ways. First, it took on board the growing dissatisfaction with how children with special needs were being educated by emphasising the collective responsibility of the whole education service. Second, it challenged the notion that special needs could be defined solely in terms of 'handicap' caused by defects in individual children.

However, because the 1944 legislation had created such a neat and easily managed system which evolved its own cadre of professional self-interest, it took over a decade for the Plowden philosophy to be felt in the area of special needs. The Warnock Committee was set up in 1974 by the then Secretary of State for Education, Margaret Thatcher, because of mounting unhappiness with the legacy of 1944. Its report was published in 1978 and is the single most important document ever produced on special needs. Much of the policy and practice of today stems from the Warnock Report because it was the more enlightened responses to its recommendations which became the best approaches encapsulated in the 1994 Code. It is interesting to note those conclusions of the Warnock Report which now underpin the philosophy of the Code of Practice. Nine in particular stand out:

- The emphasis on a wide ranging definition of SEN which is couched in educational rather than medical terms.

- The notion that up to twenty per cent of children in *mainstream* schools have learning difficulties because of SEN.

- A multi-agency approach to assessment and provision.

- The creation of a concept of a partnership with parents during the decision-making processes.

- The inclusion of children of pre-school age in the assessment procedures.

- The extension of special needs provision into further and higher education.

- The shift of focus away from the child towards factors in schools which may exacerbate the special needs. (This is why classroom organisation, staff training and teaching strategies are such important facets of each school's policy on special needs.)

- The needs of most children can and should be addressed using the resources normally available to all schools.

- Many children are not failing *in* the system, they are failed *by* the system.

Many of the recommendations of the Warnock Report found their way into the Education Act 1981. In particular the old discredited 'categories of handicap' were abolished and replaced by a definition of 'special needs' which was educational rather than medical and which placed variations in need on a continuum. Needs would now be assessed within the context of where and when they had been identified so that *all* the factors which influence opportunity and achievement were significant. Of profound importance was the realisation that pupils were not to be 'labelled' for life and that needs could vary over time and in different education and social contexts. Thus variable needs meant greater flexibility in managing resources and in determining the nature and quality of interventions. It was at this point that the procedures for the annual review of statements of SEN were introduced. The overall framework for special needs, established by the 1981 Act, was further strengthened by the Education Act 1993 and its supporting Regulations of 1994 which spawned the Code of Practice. The Code of Practice itself arose from pressure to introduce a more consistent approach to monitoring procedures before formal assessment of needs led to statements.

This 'potted history' of the development of attitudes towards special needs in the second half of the twentieth century has, of necessity, been brief. The results of much valuable research have been omitted, as have the effects of well-respected academic critiques of legislation and reports. However, one lesson is clear: the development is evolutionary not revolutionary and so must continue. SENCOs are in the vanguard of the evolution and their experiences will undoubtedly shape what is to come.

Finally, to reinforce that latter point and perhaps give a sense of direction to future evolution, SENCOs should start to use their influence to address these two fundamental issues which characterise the evolutionary stage at which we now find ourselves.

■ How can the consideration of the curriculum shift away from ensuring children's needs are *met* and move towards an analysis of how the curriculum has contributed to the *creation* of those needs? In other words making the leap away from defining special needs in terms of the child itself.

■ How can we move the response of each school and local authority away from defining special needs in terms of *provision of resources*? The old categories of 'handicap' were a convenient tool for managing resources; is not the five stage model just a variation on the same theme?

The Code of Practice explained

The Education Act 1993 charged the Secretary of State with responsibility to produce a Code of Practice for special educational needs. The previous section of this chapter explains the pressure which brought this about. In 1994 the Department for Education (now DfEE) published the Code of Practice on the Identification and Assessment of Special Educational Needs, a document which runs to 166 pages. A simplified and updated version is expected to be published in the Autumn of 2000. Also, in the light of OFSTED inspections and further studies by Her Majesty's Inspectors of Schools (HMI), reports on the progress of implementing the Code have been published. SENCOs should familiarise themselves with these additional reports because they contain many examples of the best practice observed in schools. See especially HMCI reports: 'Pupils with Specific Learning Difficulties in Mainstream Schools', and 'The SEN Code of Practice: Three Years On', both free from OFSTED.

The purpose of the Code was to issue practical guidance to local education authorities and the governing bodies of all maintained schools on the responsibilities they had towards all children with SEN which were stipulated in Part III of the 1993 Act. The main aim of the Code was to focus on provision so that schools and LEAs could obtain 'best value' from the financial and other resources available. The status of the Code is such that it assumes statutory duties will be fulfilled but offers general guidance on how this may be done. This is why everyone concerned must 'have regard to' what the Code says and must not ignore it. Underpinning the Code are two broad principles:

■ there is a continuum of special needs reflected in the full spectrum of ability so that this is matched by a continuum of provision;

■ the special needs of most children can be met in mainstream schools, with expert help if necessary.

These principles are reinforced with statutory duties imposed on LEAs, health services and social services to respond, within set time limits, to requests for formal assessments and the issuing of legally enforceable statements.

The Code begins with an affirmation of its 'fundamental principles' and these are set out in Table 3.2 on page 37. Table 3.3 on page 38 outlines the practices and procedures which are seen to be essential in meeting these principles and the Code should be studied with these kept firmly in the forefront of thinking. The synthesis of both principles and procedures, together with all the recommendations of the Code, is best shown in the advice to adopt a staged model in which responsibility gradually shifts away from the school alone, towards schools and LEAs sharing provision and assessment. As the Code is intended for guidance, there is scope for variety in the number of stages and how they are defined, but the preferred model is given in Table 3.1 which follows.

The contents of Tables 3.1, 3.2 and 3.3 are covered by Crown Copyright and are reproduced here with the permission of the Controller of Her Majesty's Stationery Office.

TABLE 3.1	Staged model for SEN continuum
Stage 1:	class or subject teachers identify or register a child's special educational needs and, consulting with the school's SEN coordinator, take initial action
Stage 2:	the school's SEN coordinator takes lead responsibility for gathering information and for coordinating the child's special educational provision, working with the child's teachers
Stage 3:	teachers and the SEN coordinator are supported by specialists from outside the school
Stage 4:	the LEA considers the need for a statutory assessment and, if appropriate, makes a multi-disciplinary assessment
Stage 5:	the LEA considers the need for a statement of special educational needs and, if appropriate, makes a statement and arranges, monitors and reviews provision.

TABLE 3.2 The fundamental principles of the Code

- the needs of all pupils who may have special educational needs either throughout, or at any time during, their school careers must be addressed; the Code recognises that there is a continuum of needs and a continuum of provision, which may be made in a wide variety of different forms

- children with special educational needs require the greatest possible access to a broad and balanced education, including the National Curriculum

- the needs of most pupils will be met in the mainstream, and without a statutory assessment or statement of special educational needs. Children with special educational needs, including children with statements of special educational needs, should, where appropriate and taking into account the wishes of their parents, be educated alongside their peers in mainstream schools

- even before he or she reaches compulsory school age a child may have special educational needs requiring the intervention of the LEA as well as the health services

- the knowledge, views and experience of parents are vital. Effective assessment and provision will be secured where there is the greatest possible degree of partnership between parents and their children and schools, LEAs and other agencies.

TABLE 3.3 Practices and procedures

- all children with special educational needs should be identified and assessed as early as possible and as quickly as is consistent with thoroughness

- provision for all children with special educational needs should be made by the most appropriate agency. In most cases this will be the child's mainstream school, working in partnership with the child's parents: no statutory assessment will be necessary

- where needed, LEAs must make assessments and statements in accordance with the prescribed time limits; must write clear and thorough statements, setting out the child's educational and non-educational needs, the objectives to be secured, the provision to be made and the arrangements for monitoring and review; and ensure the annual reviews of the special educational provision arranged for the child and the updating and monitoring of educational targets

- special educational provision will be most effective when those responsible take into account the ascertainable wishes of the child concerned, considered in the light of his or her age and understanding

- there must be close cooperation between all the agencies concerned and a multi-disciplinary approach to the resolution of issues.

The influence of the Code of Practice permeates this whole book and reference to it is made frequently in all chapters. It is an easy document to read or dip into and it is impossible to provide a detailed summary of all its recommendations. SENCOs should study the Code carefully, especially Section 2: 'School-Based Stages of Assessment and Provision', and Section 3: 'Statutory Assessment of Special Educational Needs'. These sections give comprehensive guidance on procedural details.

However, because the Code provides the main theoretical background to the work of SENCOs, and to make it easier for schools to check the extent to which they 'have regard to' the Code, Table 3.4 lists the main recommendations. Use this as a checklist to gauge school preparedness, to assess the extent to which the school has modified the original approach of the Code and to plan for future developments.

TABLE 3.4 Main recommendations of the Code of Practice – general school advice

1 The governing body shall determine the school's policy, establish staffing and funding arrangements and oversee the school's work. Governors should appoint a 'responsible person'.

2 The 'responsible person' will liaise with the LEA and other services and will keep teachers informed about children's special needs.

3 Schools will appoint an SEN coordinator or team to work with the headteacher on aspects of policy management and with teaching colleagues on the operation of the policy.

4 The SENCO will be directly responsible for coordinating provision for pupils on Stages 2 & 3.

5 Schools will adopt a 5-stage model (or equivalent) to identify general and specific needs and to ensure correct provision is made, especially the allocation of teaching and other resources.

6 Needs should be identified as early as possible using the broadest range of information available.

7 Care should be taken when identifying the needs of children where first language is not English or Welsh. Arrangements should be made to conduct assessments in community languages.

8 The school should keep a register of all children with SEN and should use a system of agreed proformas to record the steps taken to meet those needs.

9 Schools should develop and maintain a partnership with the LEA, health and social services, and other agencies to ensure a multi-disciplinary approach to assessment and provision.

10 All pupils at Stages 2, 3 & 4 (or the equivalent) should have an Individual Education Plan (IEP) which defines the area of need, sets targets for improvement and outlines guidance on teaching. All teachers should be consulted and given copies of IEPs. IEPs should be periodically reviewed.

11 Schools should consider the training needs of the SENCO and all staff, including non-teaching assistants. The SEN training policy should be part of the school development plan.

12 Parents should be involved and consulted at every stage. Parents should be provided with all available information about their child and the range of support, including voluntary organisations, available. Access to information via community languages or other communication modes must be made available.

13 Children should be encouraged to participate in decision making about how their needs are to be met. Children should be fully informed and involved at each stage.

14 The headteacher should be aware of the full range of support services available, national, local and voluntary. The headteacher should take all necessary steps to maintain the confidentiality of all health, social services and other agencies' reports on children's needs.

15 Schools must inform the LEA about all children at Stage 3. The LEA should stipulate a procedure for this. The involvement of LEA personnel in providing expert guidance to the teaching of Stage 3 pupils is not, of itself, sufficient notification.

The procedures for statutory assessment at Stage 4 and the decision as to whether the assessment eventually leads to a statement are strictly regulated by both the 1981 and 1993 Education Acts. Procedures are at times complex and seem convoluted, and many schools experience unacceptable delays in situations where a child's needs are deemed to demand more urgent attention. The national picture is somewhat patchy, with some LEAs seemingly having the resources to act more quickly than others. Although there are time limits imposed on stages of the procedures, those limits may be relaxed for a whole variety of reasons, the chief of which is not having all the necessary information. SENCOs should read and note those detailed sections of the Code which apply to Stages 4 and 5 because these are not mere guidance, they are the law. Schools should not find themselves the cause of unnecessary delays through failure to follow the procedures and should not automatically blame LEAs for perceived tardiness. Table 3.5 is a continuation of Table 3.4 and lists the main recommendations of the Code in respect of LEA responsibility for statutory assessments. SENCOs should note that even if the time limits are strictly followed there is a possible total of *seven months* between initial referral and confirmed statement – those are the rules and not the result of the LEA dragging its feet! Imagine the frustration at referring a pupil for assessment who has reached his or her fifteenth birthday!

TABLE 3.5 Main recommendations of the Code of Practice – statutory assessment

16 LEAs must make a statutory assessment of a child's needs if there has been a formal referral from the headteacher or a formal request from a parent. An assessment need not lead to a statement where, for example, the enhancement of a school's resources with a piece of equipment would enable the school to meet the child's needs.

17 Assessment may be carried out even though no action has been taken at stages 1–3. The stages are in no sense a progression along which a given individual pupil must travel. Pupils must be placed at whatever stage is appropriate to their needs. Children who are under five may be assessed at the request of health or social services departments.

18 When making a Stage 4 referral schools must submit written evidence detailing the reasons for the referral and including any medical reports, the view of parents and how IEPs have been used. The results of external professional inputs are also needed.

19 LEAs must inform parents of the proposal to make an assessment. The LEA must also inform the parents of the procedure to be followed and of the name of an officer from whom further information may be obtained. Parents should also be informed of their rights to make representations and submit evidence within a period of not less than 29 days. Parents should also be informed of the name of someone not connected with the LEA from whom independent advice may be sought. The headteacher, the social services department and the district health authority should be informed of the proposal to assess.

20 Except for special circumstances, the LEA should adhere to these time limits:
6 weeks to decide whether to make an assessment after notifying parents
10 weeks to complete assessment following notifying parents of decision to assess
2 weeks after assessment to issue proposed statement or decision not to statement
8 weeks after proposed statement to issue complete statement.

21 Any subsequent statements carry the force of law and the terms and conditions, including those for review, must be obeyed. Schools must carry out any elements of the statement which apply to them directly and fully co-operate with those agencies responsible for additional provision.

22 SENCOs can recommend the rescinding of statements.

To avoid unnecessary duplication, readers should refer to Chapter 2: 'Following appointment' for the recommendations of the Code for the role of the SENCO, and to Chapter 5: 'Methodology' for a more detailed look at IEPs and management roles.

_____ Synopsis of essential legislation _____

The previous sections of this chapter have shown how the theoretical basis for the SENCO's role is governed by the terms of the Education Acts of 1981 and 1993, the Special Needs Regulations of 1994 and those elements of the Code of Practice which carry the force of statute. Under the terms of all of these pieces of legislation LEAs are empowered to devise their own regulations in respect of the devolution of funds and the provision they make. An essential priority for SENCOs upon taking up appointment, especially in an LEA for which they have not worked previously, is to make early contact with the special needs advisor or head of support services to ascertain the nature and extent of LEA requirements which should be met.

Additionally there are other pieces of important legislation which can and do impinge upon the work of SENCOs and this brief section outlines the principal ones. (See also Chapter 7: 'Managing your inspection' – compliance with statutory requirements, page 183.)

The education system is controlled mainly by three Acts of Parliament: the Education Act 1996, the School Inspections Act 1996 and the School Standards and Framework Act 1998. These Acts consolidate the principles previously established by the Education Acts 1944, 1980, 1981 and 1986, the Education Reform Act 1988, the Education (Schools) Act 1992 and the Education Act 1993. The Education Act 1996 and the Education Act 1997 were amended by the School Standards and Framework Act 1998. Within this legislation the Secretary of State for Education and Employment has the power to issue detailed legal requirements through Statutory Instruments (SI). The Department for Education and Employment (DfEE), also known previously as DFE (Department for Education) and DES (Department of Education and Science), issues guidance by means of circulars. Three examples will suffice at this stage to illustrate the effects of this legislation on the SENCO's work.

■ At every school there should be employed a staff of teachers suitable and sufficient in number for the purpose of securing the provision of education appropriate to the ages, abilities, aptitudes and needs of the pupils. (The Education [Teachers] Regulations 1993, Statutory Instrument 1993/543.)

- LEAs are required to carry out an assessment of children with special educational needs and then to make and maintain a statement specifying the special provision required. If the name of a maintained school is specified in the child's statement the governing body of the school is required to admit the child. (Education Act 1996 and School Standards and Framework Act 1998.)

- The governing body of any school has responsibility for appropriate provision for pupils with special educational needs (Education Act 1996).

The principal areas of legislation, together with any Statutory Instruments and DfEE Circulars which may be relevant, are set out in Table 3.6 which follows. SENCOs should ensure that schools have copies of these documents for reference. The most useful reference point, which gives a comprehensive guide to the legal background to SEN, is to be found as an appendix to the Code of Practice. This is called 'The Education (Special Educational Needs) Regulations 1994' and repays careful study.

TABLE 3.6 Examples of main aspects of legislation

What must happen	Acts, Instruments and Circulars
■ Schools must pay full regard to the equal opportunities of pupils with SEN. Governors must make known the school's arrangements for admitting disabled pupils and how such pupils gain access to the full curriculum. Governors must ensure that pupils with SEN join in everyday activities with other pupils.	Disability Discrimination Act 1995 Education Act 1997 Children Act 1989 DfEE Circulars 3/97, 7/99, 8/99
■ All registered pupils must be provided with a programme of careers education between the ages of 14 and 16.	Education Act 1997 School Standards and Framework Act 1998 DfEE Circular 8/98
■ All pupils in maintained schools shall follow the National Curriculum to the maximum extent possible but its provisions may be disapplied or modified in relation to pupils with statements of SEN, except for Religious Education. Headteachers can disapply or modify the National Curriculum for pupils without statements for a maximum period of	Education Act 1996 School Standards and Framework Act 1998 DES Circular 15/89

six months. The period of disapplication cannot be extended. Governors, parents and the LEA must be informed of the arrangements.	
■ Schools have a duty to protect children from harm. Designated teachers and procedures must be in place to notify the appropriate authorities if schools have a concern about pupils' safety or welfare.	Children Act 1989
■ Schools should have assessment arrangements in place for identifying pupils with SEN which reflect the guidance contained in the Code of Practice.	Education (Special Educational Needs) Regulations 1994 Education Act 1996
■ Schools are required to keep records on every pupil and update these at least once per year. Records must be available to parents, to pupils over the age of 16, and to any educational establishment to which pupils transfer.	Statutory Instrument 1989/1261 Data Protection Acts 1984 and 1998
■ All schools are required to contribute to the annual review of pupils who have a statement of SEN.	Education Act 1996 DFE Circular 6/94
■ Approved independent schools may admit children with statements of SEN provided they meet the same standards of premises, staff qualifications, education and care as those expected in maintained schools.	Education Act 1996 Statutory Instrument 1994/651 DFE Circular 3/94

Whole school strategic management

This chapter has concentrated so far on the statutory basis upon which special educational needs are provided for in schools. This has given the SENCO the essential theoretical background to the role and explained how the SENCO's responsibilities have evolved in tandem with a more enlightened view of children with learning problems. Of equal importance, however, in establishing the theoretical parameters of the SENCO's work is how the role is perceived in individual schools, particularly the place occupied by the postholder in helping to determine how the school should develop: *the strategic management role.*

Remember that this book is intended for newly appointed or aspirant SENCOs and that established holders of the post will already have carved out a niche for themselves in the school hierarchy. Newly appointed SENCOs need to know where they stand on many issues, not the least of which is the degree to which responsibility is apportioned between those who have different roles to play. For example, the SEN governor, the headteacher, the 'responsible person' and the SENCO all have clearly defined statutory duties, but the boundaries between them are often blurred, especially if one person has more than one of these roles. It is possible, of course, in a small primary school, for the headteacher to be the responsible person and the SENCO, in which case the impact on strategic management could be considerable if SEN is treated as a significant whole school issue. On the other hand, if the SENCO role is seen purely as an administrative one then the influence of SEN on strategic decision making could be minimal. The size and type of school and the proportion of pupils with special needs are obvious influencing factors, but one thing has become abundantly clear over the past few years: the SENCO's role is expanding and evolving at a significant rate and when the policy of 'inclusion' really begins to bite the role will be pivotal. The new emerging role of the SENCO has been steadily developing for a number of reasons:

- there is now a greater understanding of the Code of Practice and the demands it makes on a wide range of skills;

- specific qualifications, training and professional development opportunities are more readily available so that a unique level of expertise can be reached;

- this level of expertise has become essential as the role of LEAs as a source of professional advice has diminished;

- far more is known about particular types of need and the very specialised resources and teaching techniques required;

- the technical knowledge required for the process of statutory assessment and statementing is considerable and SENCOs are expected to work with the LEA rather than hand over the entire responsibility;

- there is far less transference of pupils from mainstream to special schools, in fact movement is now far more likely to be in the opposite direction;

- there is an abundance of specialised testing and assessment material which must be mastered if it is not to be misused and many SENCOs have become expert at diagnosing precise problems;

- with more knowledge has come the need for more specialised resources, including information and communications technology, so expertise has had to develop;

- significant elements of the SENCO's work have brought postholders into greater contact with governors, the headteacher, the LEA and parents than experienced by any other teacher;

- the statutory entitlement of all pupils to experience the National Curriculum has challenged all traditional views on curriculum organisation for SEN pupils so the SENCO is now much more involved in curriculum planning in all subjects;

- schools are much more heavily committed to analysing assessment data, setting targets and planning for development than they were a decade ago, and these activities involve considerable expert input from the SENCO;

- there has been a massive switch of expectation of the role of the subject or class teacher. The old style response to a teacher's problem was to literally take it away in the form of special classes, withdrawal groups or sections of the school following a different curriculum. Now class and subject teachers are expected to meet the challenges themselves for which they need support and guidance from the SENCO;

- the wide variation of needs and the numbers of pupils at different stages found in some classes means that SENCOs and subject teachers have had to work much more closely together on, for example, the development and use of IEPs; and

- many schools are beginning to recognise all of the above in allocating that most precious resource – TIME – to SENCOs to enable them to fulfil the role effectively.

The latter point about having sufficient time is an important one. Not only is the routine administration time-consuming but in order to discharge the other functions of the role adequate time must be given. This is clearly easier to achieve in a large secondary school than in a small primary, but many schools are successfully creating the necessary time by looking creatively at the composition of the school day and the use of regular supply cover. The annual review of a statement cannot be 'slotted in' at the end of lunchtime! Moreover, it is incumbent on headteachers and other senior staff to review their own teaching commitments where significant responsibility is delegated to others. Newly appointed SENCOs therefore need to either secure an allowance of time specifically dedicated to the job or else make it perfectly clear what can or cannot be achieved in the time given. Although the problem of time is still present in many schools, it is a diminishing problem as more and more headteachers come to appreciate the scope of the SENCO's role.

Many established SENCOs have found that their role has significantly expanded in the last three or four years. For example:

- a SENCO in a primary school in East Sussex who has devised, and runs, a programme of in-service courses on teaching pupils with dyslexia;

- a SENCO in a middle school in Bedfordshire who has taken over responsibility for whole school literacy and numeracy;

- a SENCO in Liverpool who has been designated as a 'lead teacher' in behaviour management and works with teachers from other schools on developing behaviour management strategies; and

- a SENCO in a secondary school in the Midlands who has been handed responsibility for developing GNVQ and other vocational courses at Key Stage 4.

What this shows is that the emerging role of the SENCO is far greater than the mere filling-in of forms or updating the register of special needs. It is a matter of changing perceptions and the new SENCO needs to establish where the role 'fits' in the strategic management of the school. Job descriptions help, because they should establish the theoretical basis of the role *in that particular school*, but many schools are still not clear about the relationship between job descriptions, appraisal, targets and professional development, so there is much falling down between stools.

Both Chapter 2: 'Following appointment' and Chapter 5: 'Methodology' cover important aspects of the SENCO's possible role in whole school management issues. In this chapter it is more important to focus on the theoretical parameters of the job. Complete the task below, then refer to Table 3.7 which follows and which completes this section of the chapter. Table 3.7 is in the form of a checklist of management activities which have a bearing on whole school management. Use it appropriately in negotiations, especially over the allocation of time.

TASK 12

The developing role of the SENCO

It is essential to cultivate a good working relationship with other SENCOs in your area. Talk to them about how and why their roles in their schools have changed. Ask them particularly about how they manage their time.

TABLE 3.7 Whole school management functions checklist

SCHOOL MANAGEMENT FUNCTION	Participate in this now ✓	On current job description ✓	Need further training on this ✓	Time is allocated to this ✓	Need more time for this ✓
Development planning					
Monitoring of other staff					
Staff training, guidance, advice					
Assessment and target setting					
Liaison with LEA and professional agencies					
Curriculum planning					
Working with and reporting to governors					
Chairing and arranging meetings					
Policy development and publications					
Team building and leadership					
Organising pupil grouping					
Accommodation and resources					
Employment of staff					
Timetabling					
Finance and budget control					
Meeting with parents					

Summary

- Much of the work of SENCOs is determined by procedures laid down in regulations or statutes. Postholders who are new to the job need to gain an appreciation of the theoretical basis to their work.

- Although the Education Act 1944 established the principle of post-elementary education for all, it relegated 'handicapped' children to a very poor fourth in the pecking order and defined special needs in medical rather than educational terms.

- The Plowden and Warnock reports represented great leaps forward in educational thinking and marked the beginnings of the process now referred to as 'inclusion'.

- The Code of Practice represents the latest stage of development and defines what SENCOs must do in their own schools to identify and make provision for pupils with special educational needs. Aspects of the Code relating to statutory assessment and statements are governed by strict regulations which must be obeyed even if the time taken up seems somewhat protracted.

- Other Acts, Statutory Instruments and Circulars further define the limits of the SENCOs' responsibility and point to areas where governors and headteachers must act.

- It is important for newly-appointed SENCOs to establish the extent of their role in influencing whole school management issues. The role has developed considerably since its inception and many schools are acknowledging the emerging influence of SENCOs on issues of wider school significance.

chapter four

Policy formulation and implementation

Introduction

This chapter concentrates on Special Educational Needs as a whole school issue. All schools are encouraged to develop policies for a wide range of issues, and the advantage of a wider policy is that it demonstrates a backcloth of management processes which are designed to produce a consistent approach to important matters, ranging from the design of the curriculum to what to do if a pupil is being bullied. Children value consistency and teachers need clear guidelines for action in a system bedevilled by regulations governing nearly every facet of the job. Policies proliferate, and it is by no means certain whether all of them are actually needed: after all it is what actually *happens* that matters in a school, not a filing cabinet full of pristine policy documents. Besides which, in those schools where there is a culture of consultation and meaningful participation in management decisions, teachers will value the *process* of putting together a policy more than the policy itself. In these circumstances there will be a greater sense of 'ownership' of the decisions, there will be a recognition of the importance of the central issue, and there is likely to be a greater consistency about how the policy is put into practice.

Some school policies, however, are mandatory and a whole school policy for Special Educational Needs is one of them. Sections 323–329 of the Education Act 1996 require the governing body to determine, with the headteacher, the school's SEN policy, publish it in the school prospectus and inform parents about the success of the policy in the annual report. This chapter examines the required features of an SEN policy and provides guidance on the management tasks and responsibilities surrounding the process of writing a policy and ensuring its effective implementation.

A summary of the main management learning points is given at the end of the chapter. By following the checklists and discussion or research exercises SENCOs will be able to measure themselves against examples of best practice.

_____ Why do we need a policy for SEN? _____

Even if there were no Code of Practice, schools would still need to determine how best to identify and provide for pupils who have special needs. Circumstances vary so much between schools and there are so many organisational structures which reflect school size and type that there is no single 'correct' approach which could possibly encompass all variations. The proportion of pupils with special needs varies both in quantity and degree of severity between schools and there is always the question of how best to cater for gifted or exceptionally talented youngsters. Schools have a duty to ensure all pupils derive maximum benefit from their educational experiences so there is a clear need for a properly structured approach to how the school supports its children in their endeavours to succeed and make progress.

All schools have now taken on board the principle that the full National Curriculum in mainstream schools should be an entitlement which is only modified in exceptional circumstances and that wholesale withdrawal of groups of pupils from 'normal' lessons stigmatises them, reinforces failure and frankly doesn't work. It would be disingenuous to suggest that no child should ever be withdrawn from a lesson so that concentrated corrective or extension work can take place because this is good practice. No, what is being referred to is the old pre-Code practice of identifying a group of children, calling them 'slow learners' or 'remedial' or a whole host of more pejorative names and subjecting them to a sterile curriculum occasionally enlivened by the skill of a specialist 'remedial' teacher. The system was easy to organise and relied on setting or streaming to generate the group. The learning problems of a significant number of children were totally unknown and ignored by the vast majority of teachers in secondary schools and inexpertly addressed by class teachers in primary schools. Once discredited, that approach was replaced by something better, one that placed the needs of the pupil at the heart of the curriculum and hence at the heart of teachers' planning in all subjects. Now *all* teachers are fully involved, their work needs purpose and direction, they need to know what to do and how to act in the face of unfamiliar problems, they need guidance on developing new teaching skills and they need the security of knowing they are doing the right things. In short, the basic philosophy and approach requires spelling out in the form of a policy. And then there are the governors.

The changed role of governors has more or less coincided with the establishment of the Code of Practice. The Code came about because some schools in some LEAs had been developing a new *inclusive* approach to special needs with formal guidelines and procedures which were looked upon as models of good practice to be shared across the board. In those schools which were most effectively coping with a wide range of special needs governors had taken a particular interest and showed a strong lead when it came to securing and allocating resources. If we add on the devolution of budgets (including funding for special needs) to schools and responsibility to governors for management and control of finances then the picture is complete: governors *had* to be involved in how provision for special needs was determined in each school. Because most governors are not involved 'hands on' on a daily basis, the details of provision for special needs became, of necessity, documentary. Hence the need for a policy statement. Policy statements themselves became models of good practice so it only took a small step for the Code of Practice to advocate a whole school policy, for which governors would be responsible, as an example of best practice for all schools.

Not so long ago there was no such thing as 'special needs'. Children were 'handicapped' or 'educationally sub-normal' (ESN), or at best 'slow learners'. Little was known about the way children learnt so those pupils who failed to make the same rate of progress in an age-related narrowly conceived curriculum were blamed, ridiculed and sometimes punished. Special needs has come a long way in little over twenty years thanks largely to Mary Warnock's committee report, see Chapter 3: 'Theoretical basis' – the legacy of the Warnock Report 1978, page 34. Think of the battles to get dyslexia, dyspraxia, autism and attention deficit disorder recognised as genuine physical, psychological or neurological conditions and imagine the torture inflicted on youngsters labelled 'very naughty' or 'thick'. *Now question the need for a policy.*

The present situation, then, is the best advocate of the need for each school to have its own policy. Each school is unique and has its own values and ways of doing things: this should be the chief characteristic of a policy on anything, let alone special needs. We know that children's learning is a product of psychology, attitude, environment, teaching and the curriculum. We know that different children learn in different ways and that different subjects pose different learning problems. We know that children can have different degrees of learning difficulty and we have begun to master the techniques of identification and diagnosis albeit using some pretty crude measuring instruments. Above all, we know that every teacher, given appropriate guidance and support, can satisfactorily handle most types of special need in their own classrooms.

Finally, like so many other features of life in today's schools, special needs can no longer be kept 'in house'. There are aspects of legislation which must be obeyed – on discrimination, disability and child protection for example – and LEAs still retain funding for proportional delegation to schools or to support statements. Also there is the question of liaison with other schools and outside agencies – all requiring a particular procedure with accompanying paperwork. The complexity of the whole enterprise makes a written statement of policy inevitable, hence the statutory obligation.

TASK 13

Historical developments

By speaking to older colleagues or parents who may have attended the school, trace the history and development of special needs provision at your school.

By projecting that development forward and regarding the present situation as merely an evolutionary stage, try to anticipate how special needs provision will look in five years' time.

What changes to your current policy would you envisage as being necessary to accommodate these developments? Look especially at the use of technology.

The need for a whole school policy for special educational needs is summarised in diagrammatic form in Fig. 4.1 on page 56. Does your current policy reflect these pressures?

———— Essential steps in ————
producing school policies

A policy is a statement of how a school sees its aims and objectives being translated into practical reality. We must note at this stage that there is a difference between *policy* and *procedure*. Consider these two statements:

> *'Pupils' records will be updated regularly.'*
>
> *'Pupils' records are kept in the blue filing cabinet at the back of Mrs Green's room. Statements are separately filed in the top drawer of the locked cabinet next to it. Teachers should add test results and any termly assessment marks to each pupil's sheet for stages 1 and 2 pupils only ....'*

The first statement is policy, the second is procedure. SENCOs need to decide just how many procedural items need to be included in a policy statement because the end product could be too hefty and therefore difficult to evaluate meaningfully. In some schools where really good practice has been observed, two documents are produced: one is a straightforward statement of policy intentions, and the other is a guidance handbook which interprets the policy in terms of daily recommended practice.

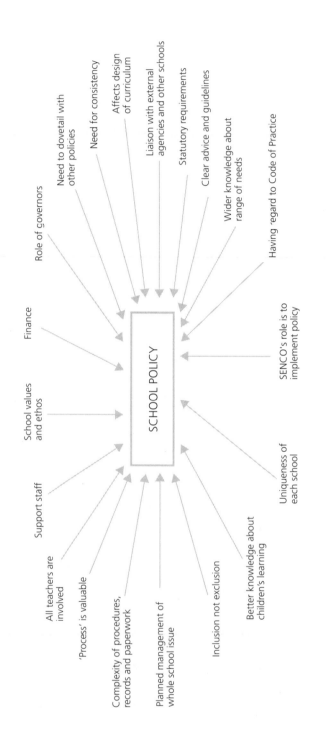

FIG. 4.1 Factors illustrating the need for a whole school policy on special needs

Role of governors

Need to dovetail with other policies

Need for consistency

Affects design of curriculum

Liaison with external agencies and other schools

Statutory requirements

Clear advice and guidelines

Wider knowledge about range of needs

Having regard to Code of Practice

Finance

School values and ethos

Support staff

All teachers are involved

'Process' is valuable

Complexity of procedures, records and paperwork

Planned management of whole school issue

Inclusion not exclusion

Better knowledge about children's learning

Uniqueness of each school

SENCO's role is to implement policy

SCHOOL POLICY

Policy or procedure

Examine your current SEN policy or one from another school carefully. Highlight statements which are policy and those which are procedure. Would a guidance handbook be a more useful version?

The worst school policies for special educational needs are those which ignore the existence of the school and simply summarise the Code of Practice; the result is that sections are written in bland generalist terms and could be applied to any school anywhere. The best policies take account of the unique nature of the school, its traditions, customs and practices, and present a picture of special needs provision which is in harmony with the prevailing 'culture' or 'value system' of the school and which reflects the school's overarching set of aims. The policy must 'have regard to' the Code of Practice, of course, but SENCOs and headteachers should always heed the good advice from our colleagues in industry: *the best policy is one that can be implemented.*

Given that the SEN policy should both reflect the requirements of the Code of Practice and be couched in terms which emphasise the school's central philosophy, there are five essential steps which need to be taken to produce a policy which is succinct, worthwhile, covers all statutory requirements and is easy to implement. Use these steps as a guide to producing a new policy or as a tool for reviewing an existing one. The steps are given in Table 4.1 on pages 58–60.

It is rare for a school not to have a formal policy for how it intends to provide for pupils with SEN. SENCOs are responsible for implementing policies and it certainly helps if they are instrumental in framing those policies. However, newly appointed SENCOs may well be pitched into situations where they are expected to put into practice policies in which they have had no input whatsoever. The problem is exacerbated where the policy is heavily underscored by procedural detail and this is another good reason to keep procedural interpretations separate so these can be modified without changing the terms of the policy itself. If a major re-writing of the policy is not possible then the new SENCO should undertake a thorough review to establish those features of the policy which indicate overall attitude and approach and those which dictate daily classroom practice. The classroom practice features are important because the new SENCO might disagree with them, or want to introduce a practice which has been observed elsewhere, and the new SENCO may, and indeed should, have new ideas.

TABLE 4.1 Essential steps

Essential step	Meaning	Effect on policy	Method
Strategic planning	Schools must plan for how the daily practices are to be maintained and for future development. Planning for development across a broad front is *strategic* planning. The SEN policy should encompass both maintenance and strategy. If there are developments in staffing or accommodation or changes to school character the policy should be able to accommodate these.	Need for widest possible consultation as part of policy making process. Responsibility for technical aspects should be delegated to SENCO but overall shape and thrust of policy needs to come from headteacher. There is also the question of 'house style' so that format and wording are consistent with other policies. SEN policy needs to 'fit' overall strategic direction in which the school is headed and not put down too many historical roots which impede development.	■ Discussions with headteacher ■ Discussions with colleagues ■ Discussions with LEA personnel ■ Scrutiny of other school policies ■ Scrutiny of development plans ■ Issuing guidance on including SEN issues in subject development plans
Relationship with key players	The SEN policy is intended for whole school consumption and also includes practical relationships with external agencies. Within the school there are responsibilities undertaken by governors, headteacher and senior managers as well as pastoral and curriculum managers. LEA staff, social services health workers and educational psychologists are also players. Liaison with other educational institutions and employees is also important.	The roles and responsibilities of all the key players need to be made explicit in the policy. Best to include key personnel twice, once as their roles arise in the main text of specific sections and again as a list of roles at the end. Of particular importance is to gain agreement beforehand on a definition of the roles to be played by class or subject teachers because policies are often too vague on this issue.	■ Review of experience of relationships with key players ■ Listing what works and what doesn't ■ Noting down clear expectations and definitions of roles ■ Present stages and formal interventions in the form of a flow chart

TABLE 4.1 Continued

Essential step	Meaning	Effect on policy	Method
School values and aims	The school should have a value system which underpins everything it does. This will be reflected in attitudes to pupils and staff, relationships with parents and liaison with the community in all factors influencing the tone of the SEN policy. The curricular opportunities and how pupils are grouped are also representative of values. Aims show us how these values become reality and are related to expectations of how pupils will turn out.	Policies should begin with a clear statement of school aims and values. It should be obvious how the policy contributes to fulfilling school aims and how the structures recommended by the Code of Practice are being interpreted to fit the context and prevailing culture of the school. It is particularly important to reflect governors' wishes or a specific denominational viewpoint.	■ Establish overall description of chief characteristic of school, is it care or academic rigour or what? ■ Examine relevance of school aims to special needs ■ Interpret school aims in terms of SEN and state in precise language ■ Harmonise with Code of Practice
Objectives of policy	The reasons for policy statements should be made clear. The main objective is to create a framework for action which covers all foreseeable eventualities. Secondary objectives will include demonstrating how cross-curricular provision will work and a series of pronouncements about pupils' learning outcomes. A separate section on objectives for gifted or talented pupils should be included as should expectations for the work of special units.	We always have to ask 'what is this policy designed to achieve?'. Also, when writing sections, the purpose of the text should be made clear. A useful phrase is 'In order to .....' and if this phrase introduces each section then the writing will have a sharper focus to it.	■ The second set of statements in the policy state the clear objectives ■ Begin each statement with an objective ■ Discuss and consult over objectives beforehand ■ Include nothing which has no purpose

TABLE 4.1 Continued

Essential step	Meaning	Effect on policy	Method
Separate procedures	Policies are statements of intent with some reference to practical application, not essays describing the status quo. Good policies give an authoritative backcloth against which to develop appropriate practices and are sufficiently flexible to allow new practice to develop without compromising the policy.	Classic 'chicken and egg' syndrome. Policy should dictate practice not the other way round. Start with what is essential and find ways to implement it, do *not* start with what you already do and seek to ratify it through a policy. A policy should not be a mere description of existing practice. Create a guidance handbook to accompany the policy which can easily be modified.	■ Review current policy for simple descriptions of what happens ■ Remove sections which simply tell people what to do ■ Reduce policy to matter of fact statement of intentions ■ Begin developing a guidance handbook

_____ The key features of a SEN policy _____

The most important aspect of the school policy is that it must reflect the work of the whole school. Although the governing body and the headteacher should take overall responsibility for its production and implementation, the school as a whole should be involved in developing the policy. Nor should the school confine itself to its own resources when addressing the issue: consultations with the LEA, local schools and the appropriate funding authorities may be needed. During any subsequent revision period it is worth remembering who was involved in the inception of the policy and arranging for similar consultations to take place. The LEA and neighbouring schools are of particular importance in the process because a central aim may be to draw up a coherent approach to special needs in a local area and the policies of several schools may need to be coordinated. A newly appointed SENCO should always visit neighbouring schools, especially those from or to which pupils transfer, in order to gain an insight into policy development on a broad front.

To reflect the whole school nature of the policy it is important that each sector of school life is included. There must be clear reference to the roles of the governing body and headteacher through to the work of the classroom assistant, with all stops in-between. It also does no harm to give a brief summary of the history of the policy's development, with particular emphasis on meetings where decisions were taken or statements ratified. This avoids dissent.

As has been mentioned in the previous section, the policy should reflect the values and aims of the school both in its introductory statements and in the tone of the main text. If the 'ethos' of the school is one where collaboration and sharing of good practice is encouraged among teachers, then this approach must be obvious in the policy. If, on the other hand, the school is large, diverse and operates through semi-autonomous departments, each with its own ethos, the policy can afford to be more prescriptive. The most commonly stated whole school aim has a variety of wording around the theme of treating all pupils as individuals and maximising the potential of each child. This is often quite a glib aim with little or no attempt to accomplish it in mixed ability classes where there is not even the pretence of differentiation in anything but outcome. However, if ever a school aim was written with SEN in mind this must surely be the one. The policy can really demonstrate the power of this aim because catering for pupils' *individual* needs is what the policy should be all about. Similarly, a school aim to provide the widest possible range of educational experiences for all pupils lends itself ideally to a special needs policy which is concerned to coordinate provision across the whole curriculum.

The SEN policy, then, provides an ideal opportunity for the SENCO and others to review the whole school aims in the light of practical implementation, and the policy should certainly begin with a reaffirmation of the aims expressed in terms of their influence over how special needs is viewed in the school. For example the statement:

> 'It is the aim of the governors and staff at St Mark's that all pupils should leave the school properly equipped for the next stage of their education and approach the Key Stage 3 curriculum with confidence'

could have pride of place at the beginning of an SEN policy with the addition of:

> 'and to this end the provision for special educational needs will focus on the skills of literacy and numeracy in all curriculum areas so that no pupil leaves the school without attaining minimum acceptable standards in English and mathematics.'

Information which *must* be included

What, then, should the detail of the policy contain? Having related the policy to the school's current aims and values, and decided how much procedural information to include, schools must then 'have regard to' the Code of Practice. The minimum policy contents are stipulated in The Education (Special Educational Needs) (Information) Regulations 1994. Mainstream schools *must* provide the information shown in Table 4.2 which follows. Use this table as a checklist to review your current policy or as a guide to the minimal statutory requirements of a new policy.

TABLE 4.2   Information which all schools must provide

Reproduced from 'Code of Practice on the Identification and Assessment of Special Educational Needs' DfEE 1994

1 Basic information about the school's special educational provision:

- the objectives of the school's SEN policy
- the name of the school's SEN co-ordinator or teacher responsible for the day-to-day operation of the SEN policy
- the arrangements for co-ordinating educational provision for pupils with SEN

- admission arrangements

- any SEN specialism and any special units

- any special facilities which increase or assist access to the school by pupils with SEN

2 Information about the school's policies for identification, assessment and provision for all pupils with SEN:

- the allocation of resources to and amongst pupils with SEN

- identification and assessment arrangements; and review procedures

- arrangements for providing access for pupils with SEN to a balanced and broadly based curriculum, including the National Curriculum

- how children with special educational needs are integrated within the school as a whole

- criteria for evaluating the success of the school's SEN policy

- arrangements for considering complaints about special educational provision within the school

3 Information about the school's staffing policies and partnership with bodies beyond the school:

- the school's arrangements for SEN in-service training

- use made of teachers and facilities from outside the school, including support services

- arrangements for partnership with parents

- links with other mainstream schools and special schools, including arrangements when pupils change schools or leave school

- links with health and social services, educational welfare services and any voluntary organisations

Information which *may* be included

Once these minimum requirements have been met, the decision must now be what else to include and in what detail. For example, there is no specific mention of how the school intends to operate the five stage model, although the second section of point 2 in Table 4.2 ('Identification and assessment arrangements; and review procedures') would seem to cover this. SENCOs may wish to expand upon this in the policy to show how the model is intended to operate in the school, with particular reference to how Stage 1 pupils are identified and at what point IEPs are drawn up and used. Also, because there is direct personal intervention by the SENCO at Stage 2 and the need for the SENCO to coordinate external support at Stage 3, it is appropriate to state the school's approach to how this will actually happen. It would seem logical, therefore, to complete the sequence by describing the school's views on the procedures for statutory assessment at Stage 4 and how Stage 5 statements will operate.

Although Table 4.2 does not mention LEAs or education psychologists *per se*, there is reference to 'partnership with bodies beyond the school' in section 3, mention of resource allocation in section 2 and of specialisms in section 1. Where the influence of the LEA on aspects of the school policy is particularly strong, this needs spelling out in the policy. Some school policies even go so far as to say how the school plans to ignore the LEA where support is seen to be particularly ineffective. Where LEA support is especially valuable, say in the quality of regular support by an advisor for special needs, the policy should be specific about how that support should operate in a formal setting as opposed to the many excellent examples of informal 'personal' arrangements which most SENCOs find so valuable.

A similar issue concerns relationships with parents. Section 3 of Table 4.2 specifically mentions 'arrangements for partnership with parents' and this is important to specify in relation to reviews of statements. However, all schools have their own systems for formal and informal contacts with parents and the policy for SEN should show how it links in with other school policies in this regard.

There is also a major difference between schools in the quantity and quality of learning support assistance available. Schools have varying attitudes to this. Some use teaching staff with comparatively 'light' timetables to give support to groups of pupils (mostly secondary schools), some rely heavily on parent helpers (mostly primary schools), some employ 'floating' teachers or use the time of senior staff, while others receive more generous support from external sources. The specific use of Learning Support Assistants in relation to pupils with statements also varies in practice between schools. All this means that the policy should reflect the school's own particular arrangements for how classroom support is organised and where it is most effectively deployed. This is the area where there is often the widest gap between policy and practice and an area of policy implementation which requires the most rigorous monitoring. If the SENCO has sole responsibility for the recruitment and deployment of classroom assistants then the system for this needs careful description in the policy.

The final decision which SENCOs need to take about what to include in the policy concerns specific guidance on the school's approach to particular categories of special need. There is wide variety in the type of need experienced by different schools. Sometimes this is a product of the school's own environment, the result of specific LEA policy or simply the burgeoning 'reputation' of the school or individuals within it for a particular skill in 'handling' pupils with particular problems. The classic examples of this are pupils with physical or sensory impairment, dyslexia, dyspraxia, emotional and behavioural problems and pupils who are especially gifted or talented. Schools often have separate policies for especially gifted pupils which outline guidance on identification, differentiation, extension and the use of resources outside the school for accelerated learning, see Chapter 5: 'Methodology' page 95. There is no problem with the concept of a separate policy for giftedness, but if there is none then the school's approach should be explained in the SEN policy. Similarly, if there is a separate policy for behaviour management or a system of pastoral support plans (PSP) similar to IEPs, then fine. Include this in the SEN policy if it is not adequately covered elsewhere.

Linked to the possible need to include SEN 'types' in the policy could be a statement about particular teaching strategies and, especially, the use of Information and Communications Technology (ICT) in learning. This last issue varies tremendously between schools and is a perfect example of the SEN policy reflecting a wider school aim.

Table 4.3 concludes this section of the chapter. It is a checklist of suggested inclusions in a school SEN policy. Use it to judge the quality of the existing policy or as a template for writing a new one.

TABLE 4.3 Key policy features checklist

POLICY ITEM	INCLUDED ✔	NOT INCLUDED ✘
Each sector of school life, including governors Summary of policy development with key decisions Implications of school values and aims Interpretations or procedural details Code of Practice statutory requirements Approach to five stage model LEA involvement Relationship with parents Deployment of learning support Approaches to categories of need Specific policy on giftedness Guidance on teaching strategies Use of ICT		

Implementation, monitoring and evaluation

The true test of the quality of any policy is the ease with which it can be *implemented*. The reality of the situation with SEN policies is quite stark: it is the SENCO's responsibility to put the policy into practice and governors must report the details to parents. The importance of seeing monitoring and evaluation as part of and not separate from the implementation process is underlined by the duty placed on governors by regulation 5 of the Education (Special Educational Needs) (Information) Regulations 1994. The governing body's report to parents *must* include information on:

- the success of the SEN policy;
- significant changes in the policy;
- any consultation with the LEA, the Funding Authority and other schools;
- how resources have been allocated to and amongst children with special educational needs over the year.

This information could be viewed as being general issues for which the whole school, in the form of its senior management, is responsible. However, in commenting on the success of the policy the governors' report should show the effectiveness of the school's systems for:

- identification
- assessment
- provision
- monitoring and record-keeping
- use of outside support services and agencies

which are all items for which the SENCO is directly responsible.

It is unlikely that a newly appointed SENCO will have to implement an entirely new policy, it is more likely that a policy is already in existence and is currently being implemented, perhaps with varying degrees of success. However, there may be changes in policy to implement which have arisen following evaluation, or the new SENCO may have a fresh approach to how special needs are managed. There is also the possibility that some form of local authority re-organisation has created an entirely new establishment from the closure or amalgamation of schools, thus providing the perfect scenario: new SENCO, new policy.

Policy implementation is not something which happens by chance, there must be a systematic approach to ensure consistency.

TASK 15

Implementing policies

DISCUSSION EXERCISE

Discuss with middle management colleagues.

Examine two recently introduced policies in your school: one which has been implemented successfully and one which has not.

Consider the features of the policies and the implementation processes which have led to success and failure.

Of course, the best way to ensure successful implementation is to involve as many people as possible in the creation of the policy in the first place: if colleagues feel a sense of ownership, implementation will take care of itself. However, that may not be possible, especially in a very large school, and a newly appointed SENCO may be inheriting a situation where a policy was imposed upon colleagues with little consultation or, more likely, the evolution of practices has outgrown the original policy by about five years.

Whatever the situation SENCOs find themselves in, the policy has to be managed, and these guidelines, which are drawn from best practice in many schools, should be followed.

- Cultivate the view that policy implementation is not like slipping the lead from a dog and letting it go, it is more like keeping the lead on and controlling movement and direction.

- Managing a policy is a daily act, or series of actions, it is not a 'one-off and hope for the best' occurrence favoured by politicians and some headteachers.

- Examine the policy carefully for two features: ambiguities and tasks. Ambiguities result from imprecise wording and lack of clarity of objectives. Sometimes people do things wrongly or fail to do them at all simply because wording has been misinterpreted. For example, how is the word 'regularly' interpreted, as in 'records regularly updated' or 'regular assessment of pupils' progress'? Every day, once a week, twice per term? Does 'be generous in the use of praise to motivate pupils' mean the same thing to the English teacher and science coordinator alike? How often have you heard in meetings 'we didn't think it meant that' or 'Oh, I see, you mean we've got to do it like that!'? Successful implementation means consistent implementation and the excuses for inconsistencies should be eliminated.

A task analysis is important because it clarifies what people are actually expected to do. Write down the principal tasks in respect of the SEN policy expected of the following people:

governors

headteachers

SENCO line manager

SENCO

subject coordinators or heads of department

class or subject teachers.

Set out your relationship with the LEA or other external agencies in the following fashion:

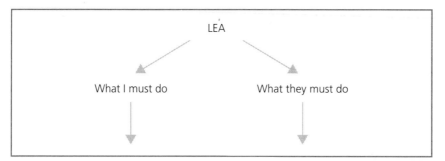

Devise a series of meetings or use the usual meeting channels to clarify everyone's understanding of the tasks and eliminate ambiguities.

■ Make sure you carry out your own tasks efficiently. So much of what others do depends upon you supplying them with accurate information and good quality advice, if you fall down on this the whole policy will suffer.

■ So much success depends upon the right guidance, so SENCOs should acquire expertise quickly through reading, attending courses and frequent meetings with other SENCOs. Become familiar with as many diagnostic testing materials as possible so that there is a battery of assessment techniques at your disposal.

■ Find ways of becoming familiar with how special needs is interpreted in each curriculum area. Being responsible for provision across the whole curriculum means knowing the problems faced in different subjects. For example, in science is pupils' progress hampered purely by literacy problems, or are there other factors to do with confidence or hand/eye coordination? Do teachers find it easier to differentiate work in some subjects compared with others? Are there some subjects where attitude and behaviour are more of a problem? Are there significant differences between subjects in the rates of pupils' progress or length of concentration span? Is it easier to use IEPs in some areas? In other words, assume nothing, *find out other colleagues' perspectives*.

■ Make sure everyone has a copy of the policy or has easy access to one. Obvious to most, but not all! Keeping SEN to the forefront is important, which is why the policy or a summary of it should be in all subject handbooks and SEN should appear in all development plans. Enlist the help of senior management in insisting upon this.

■ Consider a guidance handbook to accompany the policy in a format which follows the sections of the policy. This can be filled with useful teaching tips, differentiation strategies, suggestions for extension work, availability of resources, interpretations of assessment data, chief characteristics of types of needs, and a whole plethora of useful information which has no place in the policy but which teachers would find invaluable.

■ Set up a network of 'link' teachers for each subject area. In small primary schools everyone is the link teacher but in larger schools, and certainly all secondary schools, each department should have one teacher designated as the person responsible for monitoring special needs provision in that subject and for frequent meetings with the SENCO. In the best practice observed, the link teachers meet with the SENCO to discuss the progress of individual pupils across the whole curriculum, especially important at that crucial Stage 3/Stage 4 decision time.

■ Make sure SEN is included on the agenda of all meetings, especially those to do with the curriculum. In large secondary schools in particular there will be a preoccupation with examination results and matters affecting the majority of pupils. Do not allow special needs to become a side issue. In these circumstances really push the question of gifted and talented pupils so that you are seen to be the champion of minority interests.

■ Draw up and make widely known the rationale for the deployment of classroom and learning support assistants. You can do little about the attachment of support to statemented pupils other than ensure that it happens and make sure everyone knows the objectives of the support and targets of the statements. With other support, however, you can ring the changes so that everyone is seen to be treated fairly. Support staff should supply you with progress reports on the pupils they are helping – design a simple proforma to enable them to do this in a structured way. Also, meetings with support staff often provide valuable feedback on the picture across the whole school.

- Where procedures are complicated or need to follow a set sequence, express them diagrammatically or as a flow chart. Indicate time scales and external interventions as appropriate. These can be used to explain matters to parents as well as to locate the progress of individual pupils through the assessment/statementing procedure. The best practice I saw was a flow chart on the wall of a SENCO's office with coloured pins, representing different pupils, stuck at various points on the chart and moved when a stage had been completed.

- Finally, meet regularly with the headteacher and governor responsible for special needs. Keep the information flow active in both directions by being excited by successes and insisting on a shared responsibility for solving problems.

As you can see from this guidance schedule, the implementation of the policy is inevitably bound up with *monitoring*. However, monitoring takes three forms and SENCOs need to play a significant part in each:

monitoring of general policy application;

monitoring of a particular focal point;

monitoring of the progress made by pupils.

Monitoring the general application of a whole school policy is the responsibility of senior management and governors, not the SENCO. Naturally the SENCO will be involved in supplying information and in meeting with the SEN governor or governors' committee. Some governors embrace this role keenly, and a good example was once observed where the SEN governor was a parent governor with a son at the school who was statemented. In this instance the SENCO and SEN governor had an excellent rapport and the governor was a frequent visitor who took a particularly active role in monitoring the policy. It is difficult to monitor a philosophy, but the question is 'are all the practical manifestations of the policy happening as they should?'. The SENCO is clearly ideally placed to observe the operation of practical procedures and must be prepared to report back the strengths and weaknesses of the systems. It is relatively easy to compile an interim monitoring report, say at the end of each term, based on meetings with link teachers and support staff, and personal observation. Since the five stage model dominates SEN provision and practical measures it makes sense to use it as the monitoring model as well. Table 4.4 below demonstrates a simple template for this.

TABLE 4.4 Monitoring template

STAGE	STRENGTHS	WEAKNESSES
1		
2		
3		
4		
5		

As the previous section of this chapter shows there is much which could and should be included in the policy and any matching guidance handbook. However, it is possible to reduce all of this to three main headings:

IDENTIFICATION ———— PROVISION ———— OUTCOMES

All activities can be grouped under the appropriate title. Therefore, when it comes to completing the monitoring report proforma suggested by Table 4.4, it is a matter of concentrating on the strengths and weaknesses of each of these three aspects as they apply to each stage. This is, therefore, systematic management aimed at an important task in order to make it more efficient and easier to complete. Additionally, because the model forces the SENCO to identify where things are less than perfect, it immediately highlights the areas for the development plan, see Chapter 6: 'Setting targets to raise the standards of pupils' achievements' page 137.

The monitoring of a particular focal point is more straightforward and definitely within the remit of the SENCO. The only problem is the dilemma over the professional relationship with colleagues and this is something all managers everywhere have to learn to live with. Monitoring involves 'checking up' on the work of colleagues. Do you announce a monitoring exercise in advance and negotiate time scales and methods, thus running the risk of gaining a false impression? Or do you want to observe the real norm and be accused of conducting a clandestine operation? If you are a headteacher wishing to monitor the thoroughness of teachers' marking, do you announce this in advance or innocuously pick up exercise books at random? Which gives the truest picture, and which upsets staff equilibrium the most?

To a large degree the practical realities of the SENCO's job dictate much of this. In secondary and bigger primary schools the SENCO may have adequate time to devote to monitoring provision across the whole curriculum; in smaller schools the reality is more likely to be that the SENCO has a full-time teaching commitment and the perception of the job is someone to compile the register and fill out the forms. However, whatever the circumstances, there are things the SENCO needs to know, and it is *someone's* responsibility to ensure consistency through monitoring.

When monitoring a particular focal point, a systematic procedure is always best and is arrived at by answering these questions in Table 4.5.

TABLE 4.5 Developing a monitoring policy

What is to be the focus?	This could be an individual weakness identified in the overall monitoring, or a new procedure or a central feature of the school's approach such as the use of IEPs.
Who is involved?	This may be the SENCO alone or support staff or a member of SMT. Link teachers could be asked to investigate something and LEA staff may be involved.
What is the time scale?	An important decision to be taken in advance. Keep time scales as short as possible. A week is usually sufficient for most topics.
What methods will be used?	Discussions, questionnaires, looking at pupils' work, classroom observations, talking to pupils, assessments or tests, colleagues keeping a record.
How will the results be used?	To modify a procedure, change a teaching strategy, inform discussion, help development planning, suggest a training need.
What is the anticipated outcome?	A more user-friendly practice, greater consistency, better teaching, improvements to pupils' learning, SMT, governors and SENCO better informed.

The best practice when SENCOs are really short of time is to go in on the back of another monitoring exercise. The headteacher is going to monitor lesson planning: ask if differentiation and the use of IEPs can be looked at; there is a programme of classroom observation: ask if there could be a focus on how well support is working or how tasks are made accessible to all pupils; the LEA literacy advisor is looking at some Literacy Hour lessons: ask if pupils with SEN are coping with group work and contributing to plenary sessions. In other words, seize the opportunities presented by the many activities which are going on all the time. Smart SENCOs are not solo artists.

The monitoring of the progress made by pupils with SEN is constant and involves all teachers. Specific pupil monitoring is covered more fully in Chapter 6: 'Setting targets to raise the standards of pupils' achievements' page 142, but the purpose of monitoring in the context of this chapter is to assess the effectiveness of the policy and the practices which flow from it. It is this aspect which governors must report on, so evidence must be forthcoming. The purpose of monitoring pupils' progress is obvious and is fundamental to teaching anyway, but for this chapter the issue is a question of identifying which aspects of policy and practice account for good or poor progress so that an evaluation can be made. Try the exercise described in Task 16 below.

TASK 16

Monitoring policy effectiveness through pupils' progress

Consider two pupils, one who is making good progress and one who is not *or*, consider one pupil who is making good progress in one curriculum area and poor progress in another. If you choose two pupils, ensure that they are at the same stage on the register.

With colleagues or support staff discuss specific examples from the pupil's or pupils' work which are evidence of good or poor progress.

With reference to the policy and its attendant practices, set out the reasons for the good or poor progress in the following way. Include all factors, especially attitude and partnership with parents.

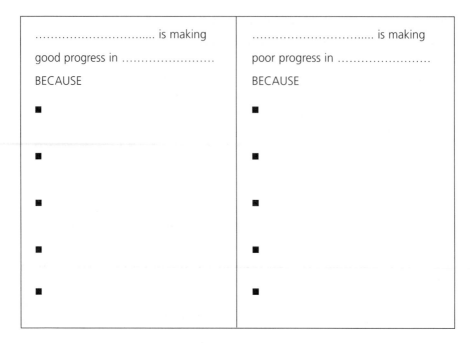

.... is making good progress in .... BECAUSE	.... is making poor progress in .... BECAUSE
■	■
■	■
■	■
■	■
■	■

Evaluation is a lot simpler than monitoring because monitoring is the spade work which enables evaluation to take place. Do not confuse monitoring and evaluation, they are not the same. *Evaluation* is making a judgement based on evidence, the evidence comes from *monitoring*. The evaluation of a policy, however, is not a question of superficial judgements, the evidence has to be measured against agreed criteria. A sprinter running a hundred metres in less than ten seconds is judged to be quick; one running it in over thirty seconds is judged to be slow. But against which standard? Suppose the second athlete is disabled, is the time still slow? Evaluation is critical in school management because it is the mid-point in the action review or planning cycles: it completes one cycle and is the starting point to the next, as Fig. 4.2 illustrates.

FIG. 4.2 The evaluation cycle

The best school or subject development plans, for example, are those which begin with an evaluation of the previous plan.

When governors report on the effectiveness of the school SEN policy they need to be making evaluative statements. Not 'we have a policy and we think it's pretty good' but 'the school's SEN policy is particularly effective in identifying the specific needs of pupils very soon after they arrive in the school. This means that reading ages improve at a fast pace and over the past three years there has been a dramatic reduction in the number of pupils scoring below Level 4 in National Curriculum tests'. Measurement against agreed criteria. It helps, of course, if the policy has clear aims and the procedures have suitable objectives, then there are criteria against which success can be measured in a process of objective evaluation.

There is nothing wrong with subjective evaluation – 'the feel good factor'. If staff have the impression that something is working well, if the SENCO feels that things are ticking over nicely but it is difficult to specify why then the evidence is a matter of teachers' professional judgement rather than something quantifiable. However, it is the quantifiable evaluations which carry more weight, none more so than better than expected improvements to pupils' learning. This, after all, is the prime objective and the ultimate test of policy effectiveness.

Like all things in management, evaluation is best conducted systematically. The policy is inextricably bound up with the practical procedures it has spawned, so focus on the areas of greatest significance over the period of a year. Table 4.6 lists some of the features which may be evaluated and the kinds of judgements which can be made. The underlying assumption behind Table 4.6 is that there are clear objectives in place behind each item and that some form of monitoring has taken place to enable the conclusions to be drawn. Table 4.6 completes this chapter; add any action points to your Personal Action Plan at the end of Chapter 2.

TABLE 4.6 Policy evaluation template

POLICY ITEM	EVALUATIVE JUDGEMENTS
Early Stage 1 identification	*Working very well. New system for SENCO visits to feeder schools picks up personal info. as well as test scores. English department now administers NFER Group Reading test to all Yr 7 in September and this gives a good indication of problems. New system of weekly progress monitoring by Yr 7 form tutors slow to develop, too paper-based. INSET for all Yr 7 and Yr 8 teachers in October very helpful in listing signs of giftedness.*
Subject-specific IEPs	
Support for statemented pupils	
Minimal paperwork	
Link teachers for all subjects	*All now in place. First meeting was very informative. Music a problem because MW is only teacher so does all dept. paperwork, need to give more support as high priority. All subject staff now familiar with register, good suggestion to use computer to identify pupils on register in each teaching group so each teacher gets a copy. English is supplying history, geography and RE with good literacy extension materials, and this has made a real difference to lesson planning.*

——————— Summary ———————

- Schools need a policy for special educational needs for statutory reasons. It is also essential that teachers understand the need for a consistent approach across the whole curriculum.

- The Code of Practice sets down the essential minimum requirements for the policy, but it is important to have a clear link with the school's values and aims.

- It is important to distinguish between policy and procedure. Policies should not be encumbered with procedural detail and a guidance handbook should be considered as an alternative. Policy should be linked also to the school's strategic planning and the roles of all parties, including those outside the school, should be made explicit.

- If SENCOs are not involved in the initial formulation of policy then they should conduct a detailed review. SENCOs are responsible for the consistent implementation of the policy and should list the tasks which each key player should perform.

- It is important that SENCOs gain an impression of how special needs is perceived in each curriculum area. The headteacher and governors are responsible for monitoring the policy, but SENCOs can and should contribute to this. SENCOs should monitor individual aspects of the policy.

- Governors must report on the effectiveness of the policy so systematic evaluation needs to be put in place. This evaluation should then be used to highlight areas for development.

Methodology

Introduction

According to one headteacher, there are three ways of doing things: the right way, the wrong way and the school way. Anything other than the school way is the wrong way! This serves to illustrate the crucial point that the circumstances in which SENCOs operate vary tremendously from school to school. In many primary schools, for example, there may be an allowance of only a few hours each week for essential administrative tasks and work on referrals or reviews is fitted in as and when necessary. In the largest secondary schools a more generous allocation of 'management' time is often offset by larger numbers of pupils with a wide range of special needs and a team of staff whose work needs directing and monitoring. Between these two poles is a wide variety of approaches and attitudes to the post determined by the structure and finances of each school. The perception of the role, therefore, will be different for each reader and, more critically, the perception of the role will be different for each headteacher.

However, some tasks and responsibilities are common to all SENCOs and the assumption behind this chapter is that the newly appointed postholder wants to be effective in the role and wants to acquire the management skills to enable the role to be taken forward. This chapter, therefore, examines and illustrates some of the essential aspects of leadership and management which SENCOs need in order to discharge their responsibilities in an efficient and effective manner. You will have to judge the extent to which each aspect applies to your circumstances and take away sufficient information for your needs.

At the end of the chapter is an examination of the list of responsibilities envisaged for each SENCO by the Code of Practice. Of equal importance is the way SENCOs go about building an effective team approach to the education of children with special needs. In addition, it is important for SENCOs to have some influence over the way talented and gifted children are given opportunities to display and stretch their abilities, so we examine those aspects of policy making which determine the school's approach to this emerging issue. It is also essential to look at how the identification of pupils' needs is translated into the sort of provision which enables each child to make the best possible progress. For all SENCOs, and especially for those whose time is severely curtailed by other responsibilities, this is a matter of the quality of communication with colleagues and we look to the Individual Education Plan to be the most essential tool in the SENCO's workshop.

As teachers begin to advance their careers by accepting or seeking posts of responsibility, an attitudinal change has to take place. There must be the realisation that the role calls for an element of leadership and management which was probably not present in previously held positions. To a degree all teachers are leaders and managers of children, but it is a different matter with professional colleagues and many teachers find the transitional period between being a 'doer' and becoming a 'persuader' difficult to cope with at first.

The most challenging phrase in the description of the SENCO's role is 'coordinating provision across the curriculum'. It is how this phrase is interpreted in each school which determines the true nature of the role. It accounts for why some primary headteachers keep this part of the job for themselves and farm out the bureaucratic chores, and for why some SENCOs have become powerful agents for change. It also accounts for how the real strength of the role has begun to emerge and why special educational needs is no longer a peripheral issue in most schools. The importance of the phrase lies in the implications for school management and curriculum organisation, and there are four elements for each school to interpret.

- The word 'provision' implies a conscious, positive and planned approach to what is essentially a reactive and at times unknown situation. It is only after specific needs have been identified that proper provision can be made so 'provision' has to be superimposed on curriculum planning which has already taken place. At times, and with some teachers or subjects, this can pose a major challenge to the SENCO. Nevertheless, children with special educational needs *must* be provided for in specifically determined ways and not left to flounder.

- By focusing on the *whole* curriculum the implication is that the issue is one which the whole school must address through every subject and every teacher. Does each teacher have the right knowledge, skill and expertise for this? Is awareness of the nature of needs and appropriate strategies sufficiently high? Is a suitable range of resources available in every lesson? Is the National Curriculum sufficiently flexible for proper differentiation to happen? Have we planned our approaches to literacy and numeracy to account for the present (and future) ranges of ability? How do we find the answers to these questions?

- The word 'coordinate' is used instead of 'manage' because it leaves room for important decisions about the curriculum to be taken elsewhere and at a more senior level. The implication is that the SENCO needs to have a finger in every subject's pie and also expects to have some influence over aspects of school life outside the taught curriculum – extra-curricular activities for instance. The key is *consistency*. SENCOs need to be sure that pupils' needs are being consistently catered for in all subject areas and this implies adequate time for monitoring. In some instances coordination means that different contributions made by different subjects are synthesised into a common objective, for example, where behaviour, concentration or presentation may be the issue rather than a specific learning problem.

- The whole phrase focuses on methodology in a very clear statement. The implication is that if some children are experiencing problems with the curriculum then the solution lies in the curriculum and not in the children. It is every child's right to have access to success and it is every school's obligation to create the conditions for success to occur. Defining that success and creating those conditions are the SENCO's prime responsibilities.

This analysis of the cornerstone of the SENCO's role makes it perfectly clear that the key to effectiveness lies in establishing strong professional relationships with colleagues at all levels, and newly appointed SENCOs need to make this their first priority. The section on team building which follows this introduction explores this issue further and its inclusion as the first section of the chapter emphasises the priority status of the topic.

It is also clear that the relationship with senior management, and in particular the headteacher, is absolutely crucial. Not only are there aspects of overall management of special educational needs which lie firmly within a headteacher's responsibility and which therefore require there to be continual liaison with the SENCO, there are also areas where responsibility begins to overlap and it is easy for potential battlegrounds to develop over such issues as priorities for staff training, the employment of support staff and the allocation of extra resources during the school year. Newly appointed SENCOs need to establish exactly where their responsibilities begin and end, but at the same time they need to ensure that senior managers live up to the SENCO's expectations. It is not within the SENCO's power, for instance, to insist that SEN figures in departmental development plans, but it is within *someone's* power to do so. Likewise, when it comes to dealing with outside agencies like the local authority, 'clout' is very important!

Actions speak louder than words, so if SENCOs really want to establish the headteacher's perception of special needs, apply the 'TWIRL' test.

TASK 17

The 'TWIRL' test

Answer these questions.

What is the headteacher's attitude towards **T**raining for teachers and others in SEN related topics?

Is it clear from development planning, meetings and general staff attitudes that SEN is a **W**hole school issue?

Is the headteacher's personal **I**nvolvement in monitoring the effectiveness of the SEN policy satisfactory?

Is there an enlightened and generous allocation of **R**esources?

Does the **L**ocation of any SEN base, office or classroom tell you anything?

———— Team building ————

It is essential to regard the SENCO as the leader of a team of fellow professionals. If SEN is truly regarded as a whole school issue then the 'team' will be the whole staff, but this may be too unwieldy a concept in a very large school. Whatever the size and type of school, however, it is important that children's needs are communicated and then provided for in a coherent and coordinated fashion, and teamwork is the approach which works best. In many schools there are likely to be a number of teams for which the SENCO has responsibility:

■ *the policy management team* – consisting of a governor or governors' committee, the headteacher and the SENCO;

■ *the support team* – consisting of the SENCO and all classroom assistants or learning support staff;

■ *the statement review team* – consisting of the SENCO, possibly a member of the senior management team, class tutor or other pastoral staff and representatives from outside the school such as parents, educational psychology and social services personnel;

- *the curriculum link team* – consisting of the SENCO and representatives from each subject or curriculum area; and

- *the learning support team* – consisting of the SENCO, other special needs teachers, the coordinator responsible for gifted pupils, staff responsible for special units and teachers employed to support pupils for whom English is an additional language.

This list will vary with circumstances and it is likely that in a small primary school the only team will consist of all other teaching colleagues and learning support assistants.

A 'team' is basically a group of people brought together to accomplish a task or series of tasks. To be effective the team must share common objectives. However, the key component of effective teams – selection of team members – is often not an option for SENCOs and so the ideal mixture of team 'types' or personal characteristics of the sort which is exemplified in the research of Meredith Belbin (1981) is present only by coincidence. The essence of Belbin's research is that the technical knowledge of team members is of secondary importance, it is the way members react to each other that counts most and this interaction is most successful where team members adopt certain roles. Three examples will suffice to illustrate team 'types':

- the *implementer* – is the person who is adept at translating theories and plans into practical working reality and has good organising skills;

- the *coordinator* – is the one who values all contributions equally and has a good grasp of the strengths and weaknesses of the team as a whole;

- the *plant* – is the team member who is always innovative and has the drive and energy to seek imaginative solutions to the team's problems.

People may, of course, adopt more than one role and may vary their roles in different circumstances according to expectations. It is a good idea to observe these roles as they exist in current teams throughout the school and SENCOs are ideally placed to do this because they are often members of a variety of pastoral, academic and management teams. It is a question of judging which teams work well together and which do not, and why. Successful team leaders know what makes teams effective and a good place to start for new postholders is real and existing teams in schools rather than theoretical constructs.

TASK 18

Existing team effectiveness evaluation

Consider two teams of which the SENCO is a member but whose prime purpose is not SEN issues. These could be pastoral, curriculum or school management teams. Try to answer the following questions.

What are the main strengths and weaknesses of the way the teams are composed and how their meetings are conducted?

Is there a clear sense of shared purpose, of common objectives and a universal agreement with the reason for the team's existence?

What proportion of the time is taken up with routine administrative matters as opposed to real debate about fundamental issues?

What examples can be given of team decisions which have made a profoundly positive difference to some aspect of school life?

What different roles do team members play during the course of a meeting or in preparing for a meeting?

What are the attitudes of team members towards decisions taken, once the meeting has finished?

If a team is given a specific brief, say to produce recommendations or come up with a solution to a problem, how does the team tackle the task? Are there clear expectations and pathways, and if so, who devises them?

What difference would it make if the teams ceased to exist?

In most school situations teachers find themselves working together for a whole variety of reasons but still spend the majority of their time isolated from colleagues because they are with groups of children. This is why it is not necessarily the team itself that matters, rather it is the strength of the team's values and objectives that are carried through into each individual's daily practice which characterise the team's effectiveness. Newly appointed SENCOs should therefore note that team building is not just a matter of how colleagues act *collectively* in the face of a common problem, it is how common objectives are interpreted by individuals in a coherent fashion which matters most.

So, how do we go about building a successful team?

CASE STUDY

'David'

David was appointed SENCO of a large primary school two years ago with the specific brief of cultivating a 'team' approach to special educational needs where previously there had been none. The three learning support assistants and four classroom assistants did not feel part of the school staff and rarely visited the staffroom. The headteacher suggested that David began by forming a working group with subject coordinators and the deputy head but he rejected that idea, instead calling for 'volunteers' during a staff meeting where he had presented a well reasoned case for a whole curriculum approach. He also explained that the terms of reference for the group would be an active workshop approach to curriculum development rather than a conduit for transferring administrative information. Routine information would be transmitted on a 'need to know' basis and through a fortnightly bulletin. All learning support staff would automatically be part of the group and to achieve this David re-negotiated the days when two part-time assistants attended the school. The team has now been working successfully for six terms. There is greater curriculum continuity between Key Stage 1 and Key Stage 2, support staff are involved in lesson planning from the outset and a major recommendation for setting for the Literacy Hour has been adopted leading to the development of a wide range of resources and increased participation by SEN pupils in plenary sessions. Of most significance is the current work on redefining the core skills of each curriculum area which is feeding into curriculum planning for topic work in Key Stage 1.

The importance of good leadership

A major feature of this short case study is that it illustrates the importance of clear *leadership* in the building of successful teams. Much has been written about leadership styles in education but this literature has tended to focus on the work of headteachers and other senior staff. Indeed, in his book *Managing Professional Teachers* (1995) Nigel Bennett demonstrates clearly that 'leadership' is rarely mentioned in the job descriptions of middle managers and that the perception of leadership by middle ranking postholders in schools tends to be that of enabling colleagues to participate in the decision-making process rather than in establishing specific directions for development. However, leadership style is important at all management levels and research has shown that the style which values and encourages *participation* in the decision-making process is ultimately the most successful. Table 5.1 summarises the research into the chief characteristics of effective team leaders. Use it as a checklist to measure your own stage of development.

The majority of experienced SENCOs, however, do not place leadership very highly on their list of the personal qualities which have earned the most respect from colleagues. Status, they say, derives from knowledge rather than position so that the advisory role is seen to be paramount and this role is most obviously manifested in the team setting. Nevertheless, if leadership is to be defined as setting clear educational goals and determining the direction to be taken in accomplishing those goals rather than as simply directing the work of others, then SENCOs have an obvious leadership responsibility. In terms of team building this means that leadership is best shown by the precision by which the objectives of the team are defined. Moreover, there should be a clear link between the objectives of the team and the objectives of the SEN development plan so that coherence is given to management process. For example, one of the prime objectives of the team should be to determine the objectives of the development plan, and one of the objectives of the development plan should be to promote teamwork.

TABLE 5.1 What makes a good team leader?*

Good motivator

- Confident

- Enthusiastic

- Fair

- Trusting

- Constructive

- Praising/rewarding

- Exemplar

Good communicator

- Assertive (able to challenge others non-aggressively)

- Listens to others

- Democratic

Good planner

- Knows own objectives

- Helps others to know their objectives

- Good at organising and coordinating

- Versatile and flexible

- Delegates effectively (right task to right person; gives support; monitors; gives feedback)

- Manages time effectively

---

* Source: Centre for Research in Teaching, Birmingham University

Team authority

Eminent exponents of the value of teamwork in the management of educational institutions like K B Everard (1990) and J Adair (1983) stress the importance of defining the terms of reference of the team and establishing the extent to which the team has the authority to take decisions about its own work. SENCOs may have only limited control over this but the question of authority is crucial. Teams which are composed on the basis of status in the hierarchy, such as heads of departments in secondary schools, may well have considerable authority but are seldom used for constructive debate on developmental issues – what they gain in status they lose in accomplishing objectives. Smaller task teams originating from and reporting to heads of departments' meetings tend to be more effective because the focus is on the task rather than on the status of the group.

TASK 19

Purpose of heads of department/subject coordinators' meetings

For what purpose do subject leaders meet in your school?

If you remove giving and receiving routine information, what is left?

What essential steps in curriculum development have been taken as a result of debate in these meetings?

How many meetings are held to ratify or gauge reaction to decisions already taken by senior management?

Subject coordinators in primary schools tend to be more effective as a group than their head of department counterparts in secondary schools. This is partly to do with the size of the group and partly because lack of time for management issues lends a sharper focus to discussions. More important, however, is the fact that each contribution has a direct effect on the daily work of each member of the group because each is both specialist and generalist in class teaching. SENCOs in all phases should look to the primary school model in building their teams because the terms of reference for the team's work need to be couched in language concerned with common approaches to teaching skills across the curriculum. In other words, the team needs to find its common ground rather than highlight its differences, and in primary schools the common ground is the response of each class to the whole curriculum. In a secondary school heads of department meeting the common ground is far more likely to be procedural rather than educational.

If the SEN team is to have its nominal status reduced because its members have a commonality of interest and knowledge rather than a position of seniority in the hierarchy, then from whence does it derive its authority? First, and most importantly, authority derives from the SENCO's own responsibilities. As seen previously the responsibility for implementing a whole school policy carries its own implicit authority which is shared with the headteacher, so there is a clear line of accountability from the team to the school's senior manager. SENCOs need to establish this from the outset and insist that the work of the team is directly reported to the headteacher and governors and not routed via another, supposedly higher status, representative group. Second, authority is rooted in the need to coordinate provision across the whole curriculum and this should be the main term of reference when setting up the team, not routine administration. Third, authority derives from the nature of the institution as a whole, its management 'style'. (For a further exploration of personal authority and management style see 'Tailpiece', page 205.) Most schools are bureaucratic hierarchies which harness the skills and knowledge of 'functional specialists' towards the achievement of institutional goals. It is the need for colleagues at all levels to defer to the specialist knowledge possessed solely by the SENCO that gives legitimacy, and hence authority, to the team's pronouncements. Some schools, though, are moving towards a more collegial approach, especially with the creation of the larger and 'flatter' leadership group, and it is in these institutions where authority as well as responsibility are delegated to autonomous units within the framework.

In practical terms, the authority of the team will be embedded in its frame of reference. For example, a team set up to:

> *'adapt the National Curriculum programmes of study and compile materials which reinforce the teaching of key skills in each curriculum area'*

will operate very differently from one which is constituted to:

> *'make recommendations to subject coordinators on a range of teaching strategies in their subjects'.*

As in most aspects of management the key is in the preciseness of the language used to describe the objective and in how ambiguity is negotiated out of the system. Successful teams know what they are doing and why they are doing it, so it is up to the SENCO to negotiate the precise terms of reference for the team with the headteacher, who then publishes them.

Team performance

One of the main problems faced by newly appointed SENCOs is a feeling that the team is not getting anywhere and is failing to 'gel'. This is sometimes the fault of imprecise team objectives or a lack of time for the team to reflect on its methods. All individuals and teams need the 'reflective' time to assess strengths and weaknesses and explore the processes by which objectives have or have not been accomplished. The wise manager builds this review time into team meetings. The failure to unite successfully is, however, quite normal in the development of teams. In 1965 B W Tuckman observed the work of small groups in organisations and noted five stages of development through which teams progressed as they acquired the experience of working together. SENCOs should not disband or re-form teams on the basis of a temporary perceived lack of unity. SENCOs, like all team leaders, need to assess the current 'health' of team development. Table 5.2 which follows lists the characteristics of effective teams and at the same time gives some broad pointers as to how successful teams are managed.

TABLE 5.2   Team effectiveness criteria

Research has enabled the characteristics of effective teams to be listed and tested. Below are the most frequently observed aspects of successful teams. As a team discuss each item and score your team accordingly.

	HIGH 1 2 3 4 5 LOW
■ Members are committed to teamwork and shared values.	
■ Coalitions and favouritism are explicitly avoided.	
■ Leader pays particular attention to building a shared culture.	
■ Members bring a range of knowledge, skills and attitudes to the team.	
■ Objectives are clear, precise, shared and understood.	
■ All members are encouraged to contribute fully.	
■ Decisions are taken and fully supported by all.	
■ Private and public attitudes and opinions are consistent.	
■ The effectiveness of the team is monitored and evaluated.	
■ Decisions are the result of debate on individual views.	
■ The need for consensus does not inhibit personal disagreement or opinion.	
■ Mutual respect means disagreement concentrates on issues not personalities.	
■ The focus of major decisions is on improvements to teaching and learning.	
■ Help is always given when requested.	
■ Delegation of tasks avoids making unreasonable demands on individuals.	
■ Colleagues are treated with fairness and trust.	
■ Opinions are respected, tolerated, and heard in full even if contrary.	
■ The leader concentrates on creating the conditions for success.	
■ The team meets regularly and has properly structured discussions.	
■ Team members respect the individual roles each is expected to carry out.	
■ Deadlines are always met by all members.	
■ Decisions made by the team are implemented consistently.	
■ Members derive strength and comfort from being part of a team.	

CASE STUDY

'Alison'

Alison is a SENCO in a medium-sized secondary school in the South West of England. The curriculum organisation of the school is based on setting in all year groups, so she and two colleagues spend most of their time supporting the teachers of the 'lower ability' sets. One group in Year 9 was causing particular concern, primarily because four pupils out of fifteen were statemented for reasons of emotional and behavioural difficulty. Alison and her team found themselves spending an increasing amount of time supporting the teachers of this group by withdrawing certain pupils and this was seen to be a cosmetic 'quick fix' to bring temporary relief. The solution was to set up a 'case conference' team which comprised all the teachers of the group, the Year 9 pastoral head and a local authority advisor with behaviour management experience. The group met three times and talked through those aspects of the curriculum and teaching strategies which had the most and least effect on the motivation of the pupils. Streamlined IEPs were produced together with Pastoral Support Plans and an agreed common set of definitions for acceptable behaviour. There was no need for the team to meet more than the three occasions, and Alison has subsequently set up other *ad hoc* teams to tackle a range of issues.

The clear message from this case study is twofold:

1 There was the expectation that the SENCO could exercise a fair degree of autonomy in devising the means by which a problem could be solved.

2 The team had a very specific objective, with each member having a stake in the quality of the outcome.

The SENCO's responsibilities as team leader

The prime management responsibility of the SENCO is to train the team to adopt a systematic approach to meeting clearly defined objectives. This is particularly important in schools where the opportunity to work together as a group is limited and yet the *team's* goals and strategies must operate in a variety of *individual* circumstances.

Training day exercise – designing forms

Spend part or all of a school training day on the following exercise.

Gather together either the regular SEN team or compose a task group. Learning support staff should automatically be part of the group.

Using the headings 'lesson planning', 'lesson support log' and 'IEP progress report', give the group the task of producing 'user friendly' proformas which will demonstrate the extent to which support staff are involved in lesson preparation, the nature and extent of support given to pupils, and the progress pupils are making towards IEP targets.

The purpose of this or any other similar suitable exercise is to promote a collaborative approach to an achievable objective which has a practical application to the daily work of colleagues.

The management responsibilities of SENCOs in the process of team building can now be expressed as a series of principles. These principles apply equally to setting up new teams or rejuvenating old ones and can be used in the smallest or largest of schools. The principles are listed in Table 5.3 which follows.

Finally, it is important for newly appointed postholders to realise that successful team building is a process which has no finite product – in essence there is no such thing as the 'ideal' team. Some colleagues are good 'team players' and some prefer to approach their own problems in an individualistic and intuitive way. Experienced SENCOs who work through teamwork are never satisfied with team performance and have ways of knowing what needs intervention and fine-tuning. The following task is based on a discussion with two SENCOs who were both asked the question ' how do you know if your team is working well?'.

Knowing your team

How do you respond to these statements about the SEN team?

	YES	NO
All of my team have a clear vision of our objectives.		
Everyone in the team can tell you specifically what we are hoping to achieve in the long and short term.		

Everyone knows what they have to do this term in order for us to achieve our targets.		
I have a clear vision of the process we have planned.		
I regularly reinforce the process we have planned by acknowledging progress.		
I have effective strategies to monitor progress of our planned objectives.		
We are all clear about how we are working towards making our school more effective.		
I can tell you what I did this week towards our team objectives.		
What action will you take if you have answered 'No' to any of the above statements?		

TABLE 5.3 Team building – management principles

1 SENCOs should exercise control over team membership. Support staff should automatically be members. Teaching colleagues should be members for what they can contribute, not for how well they receive and communicate routine information.

2 SENCOs need to establish the authority of the team with the headteacher and ratify the shortest possible route for communicating decisions and recommendations.

3 Teams should have clear terms of reference for their existence. Ideally these should be linked to an aspect of the SENCO's personal responsibility such as monitoring an item of whole school policy or coordinating provision across the curriculum.

4 From those terms of reference clearly stated objectives will follow to guide team members in collective discussions and to establish a commonality of approach outside team meetings.

5 SENCOs should build in time for reflection and review so that the strength and stage of development of the team can be assessed and methods modified to promote greater effectiveness.

6 Leadership style should promote and value participation and collaborative working and be based on the notion of the functional specialist disseminating specialist advice.

7 Short time-limited tasks help to breed a spirit of cooperation and a sense of fulfilment, especially if the tasks are designed to streamline an aspect of daily practice.

8 SENCOs should control meetings and not be controlled by the requirement to hold them. Meetings should have a clarity of purpose which is linked to improvements to teaching and learning and not to routine administrative matters.

9 Teams should be invited to describe their own success criteria because they will more readily accept essential monitoring processes.

10 The objectives of the team should be compatible with the objectives of the SEN development plan so that the whole team can contribute to the monitoring of the plan's implementation.

Giftedness and policy making

The pressure on schools to have an explicit policy on the education of gifted or talented pupils is much more recent than the impetus provided by the Code of Practice for an overall policy for special educational needs. Newly appointed SENCOs may therefore be in an advantageous position to contribute to the process of formulating a new policy. This section of the chapter looks briefly at some appropriate content for a policy for very able pupils and outlines the theory behind the management processes involved in policy creation.

In many schools responsibility for the education of the 'gifted' child does not lie with the SENCO, yet these pupils do have special needs and require the support of specialist inputs and a differentiated curriculum. In many ways these pupils embody the central philosophy of this book in that it is the *curriculum* which has to be managed to meet needs rather than the pupils. It is a description of how the curriculum is to be managed which is the chief characteristic of both a special needs and a giftedness policy.

While there is no such thing as an 'ideal' policy, the following outline should serve as a useful 'model'. It is based on the policy produced by a school in North-West London which itself derived from research into the education of very able pupils.

Assuming that the process of defining the need for a policy has been accomplished, and that in management terms what is produced is seen initially as a draft for discussion and amendment prior to adoption, policies need to begin with a description of the *background*. This can be a reaffirmation of the school's commitment to equal opportunities and usually emphasises the importance of maximising the potential of each individual child. There then follows a statement of the purpose of the policy, for example:

> *'This policy seeks to establish a more rigorous, systematic and effective response to the challenge of providing for the very able.'*

The background section is completed by a clear statement of how specific subject policies underpin the whole school approach. Primary teachers may argue for a 'whole child' approach here rather than a secondary subject model, but the curriculum itself is subject based and gifted children display their talents in different ways and in different subjects. A 'whole child' policy works well for pupils whose all-round performance is well above average, but has little relevant application for a child who is average at English yet supremely talented in mathematics, music or art.

The policy then needs to specify its *aims* clearly and unambiguously. The aims should centre around the identification of gifted and talented pupils, how they are to be provided for, supported and guided, and how talent is to be recognised and celebrated. For example, the school aims to:

> *'provide such pupils with an appropriately challenging education, and opportunities to develop their particular talents, to ensure that their potential is translated into performance.'*

These general introductory sections to the policy should now be supplemented by specific *definitions* so that colleagues are comfortable with the terminology and so that the policy can begin to have a specific focus. All research into the management processes involved in policy making, and notably the research of Baldridge, J V et al (1978), stresses the importance of the management role in ensuring that policies have a specific rather than a generalised focus which commits the organisation to one set of goals and values. Examples of such definitions would be:

the gifted – a small number of pupils who are exceptionally able in a number of areas; and

the talented – a larger number who are particularly able in a specific curriculum area.

The exceptional ability which may be found in the intellectual, aesthetic, creative, social and psychomotor fields also needs illustration with examples.

The next section of the policy should outline the methods which will be used for the *identification* of gifted and talented pupils. This will include testing and assessment procedures, records from previous schools or key stages, teachers' observations and a possible 'what to look for' checklist of the type exemplified in Table 5.4 on page 98. As with the identification of pupils with other special needs, it is the range of information which is used to form conclusions that is important rather than generalised observations. This leads naturally into an outline of suggested *strategies* for teaching and learning. A whole school policy cannot dictate the methods to be used in each subject but it can dictate that the coordinators for each subject examine their schemes of work and procedures for grouping pupils. It is appropriate, however, for the policy to outline different forms of differentiation such as differential grouping, differentiated tasks and the use of differentiated resources for learning. In this respect research into learning styles has shown that three strategies are particularly effective but that managers need to seek the commitment of teachers before they are tried. These are:

- *horizontal enrichment* – whereby the skills and knowledge learned in the standard curriculum are applied in the new and challenging contexts with a clear purpose. This is another form of planned extension work but not simply more work of the same kind already covered.

- *vertical enrichment* – whereby pupils progress to new skills at a faster pace than other pupils but remain within the standard curriculum and year group. National Curriculum level descriptors are the ideal vehicle for this.

- *acceleration* – based on the work of Gardner (1993) into multiple intelligences and Smith (1996) into a seven stage accelerated learning cycle, this depends on a careful analysis of the social well-being of the child because it entails moving through the key stages at a pace not related to chronological age until the child reaches a level more suited to his or her abilities. It also entails a teaching method which stresses a very wide range of resources and time for the pupil to assimilate and reflect.

A policy which advocates these methods must be carefully researched and introduced by managers so as to minimise disruption to other pupils.

TABLE 5.4 'What to look for' checklist

The following is a list of the chief characteristics of very able, talented or gifted children.

- Possess superior powers of reasoning, of dealing with abstractions, of generalising from specific facts, of understanding meanings and of seeing relationships.
- Have a great intellectual curiosity.
- Learn easily and readily.
- Have a wide range of interests.
- Have a broad attention span which enables concentration on and perseverance in solving problems and pursing interests.
- Are superior in the quantity and quality of vocabulary compared with children of a similar age.
- Have the ability to produce work independently.
- Have learned to read well before school age.
- Exhibit keen powers of observation.
- Show initiative and originality in intellectual work.
- Show alertness and speedy responses to new ideas.
- Able to memorise and recall quickly.
- Have a great interest in the relationship between Man and the Universe.
- Possess unusual imagination and creativity.
- Follow complex directions easily and find short cuts quickly.
- Are rapid readers with high levels of comprehension.
- Have several hobbies, many of which are academic in nature.
- Have reading interests which cover a wide range of subjects.
- Make frequent and effective use of libraries, the Internet and other information sources.
- Are superior in mathematics, especially investigation and problem-solving.

N.B. These are personal characteristics. Children displaying many or some of these qualities may, in fact, be underachieving in school work which is why achievement must not be the only determinant of talented or gifted pupils.

The penultimate section of the policy will be a statement of how *additional resources* can be used. These could include extra curricular activities, external agencies and other educational establishments. It is in this section that the opportunities for staff development can be highlighted.

The final section of the policy will detail the *monitoring* arrangements. Experience has shown that simply identifying the person(s) responsible for monitoring is not sufficient and that the success of policies ultimately depends on the rigour with which their implementation is checked. Monitoring procedures will therefore include not only who is involved but the methods to be used and the timescales involved. In this instance recording the results of conversations with pupils and parents could be important as well as the process of analysing assessment data and setting targets. As with all whole school policies the responsibility of senior managers for classroom observation, for example, needs explicitly stating. The best policies spend almost as much time explaining monitoring arrangements as they do on the policy detail itself. Table 5.5 below summarises the main headings for a policy for gifted and talented pupils.

TABLE 5.5 Policy headings

Background	–	the need for and purpose of the policy
Aims	–	what the policy is designed to achieve
Definitions	–	narrowing the focus
Identification	–	the range of information available
Strategies	–	commitment to new methods
Additional resources	–	what else can be used
Staff development	–	specific training identified
Monitoring	–	how and by whom

'Gap theory'

The theories behind successful formulation and implementation of policies are inextricably linked to the characteristics of different organisations and their approach to change. The role of the SENCO as an agent of change is referred to in more detail in a later section of this chapter and further developed in the Tailpiece, see page 208. It is important, however, to begin with a clear definition of what we mean by a policy, partly because schools have scores of them and partly because of what is known as the 'gap theory'. Originally used to analyse conflict as a problem-solving tool, 'gap theory' can be applied as a measure of management effectiveness in monitoring the implementation of a policy. Given that there is always some gap between policy and practice, the size of the gap is determined by monitoring so that both the policy and the management of it can be evaluated. Figure 5.1 illustrates the theory by showing three models. In model A the situation is almost too good to be true and indicates either excellence of policy construction and management or that the issue is a matter of low-level procedure which everybody takes on board willingly. In model B the situation is 'normal' in that some aspects of the policy are not being followed and monitoring is not sufficiently rigorous (for example, some lessons are planned with scant regard for differentiation and lesson observations are not picking this up). Model C shows glaring faults with the policy, teachers' perceptions of its 'worthwhileness' and a lack of any attempt to guide and monitor its implementation.

FIG. 5.1 'Gap theory' models

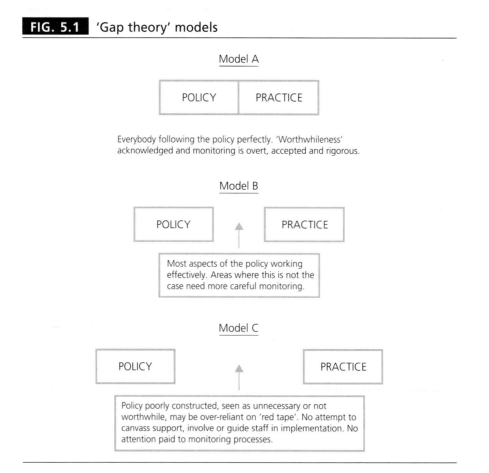

Model A

| POLICY | PRACTICE |

Everybody following the policy perfectly. 'Worthwhileness' acknowledged and monitoring is overt, accepted and rigorous.

Model B

| POLICY | PRACTICE |

Most aspects of the policy working effectively. Areas where this is not the case need more careful monitoring.

Model C

| POLICY | PRACTICE |

Policy poorly constructed, seen as unnecessary or not worthwhile, may be over-reliant on 'red tape'. No attempt to canvass support, involve or guide staff in implementation. No attention paid to monitoring processes.

A policy is a statement of intent which arises from a clearly perceived need and which involves an element of change. To be successful policies should pass the 'worthwhileness' test expressed in terms of demonstrable benefit to teaching and learning or to the overall efficiency of the organisation. In addition, a policy is the means by which the aims of the organisation are translated into practical reality so that each policy is a reaffirmation of those aims.

TASK 22

The 'worthwhileness' test

Think of a policy introduced during the past two years.

What is the *intention* of the policy?

Upon what *need* was it based?

What *changes* have resulted from the policy?

What are the tangible *benefits* arising from the policy?

To which school *aim* is the policy linked?

Has the policy been '*worthwhile*' in cost-benefit terms?

The organisational structure

In amongst all the theories of organisational structure in relation to schools, two stand out as being closest to reality. In the *political model* decisions are taken and policies are created through negotiation and trading. Alliances develop across curriculum boundaries and the objectives which lead to policies are championed by particular interest groups. Tension and conflict are seen to be normal and power lies in the hands of dominant groups rather than with formal hierarchical leaders. The focus is on the activities of *groups* rather than on the whole school and policy making is a product of the interaction between groups. Many secondary schools in particular fall into this category, with the power bases carefully constructed by heads of departments being either a strong lobby for change or the retention of the status quo. Political models are best exemplified by the following characteristics:

- conflict between the leaders of groups for influence and power, such as that between 'academic' and 'pastoral' leaders;
- individuals pursing a variety of personal and professional interests within the organisation;

- separate group commitments to a particular teaching style, means of pupil grouping or method of curriculum planning;

- differences in aims and values between groups which may be temporarily shelved in the pursuit of policies which reflect joint interest;

- overall institutional goals which are hotly contested and lead to conflict between groups; and

- policies arising as a result of pressure from one dominant group and not necessarily related to the aims of the whole school.

In schools which display the characteristics of a political model the processes of policy making will assume the shape illustrated by Fig. 5.2.

FIG. 5.2 Policy making in 'political' institutions

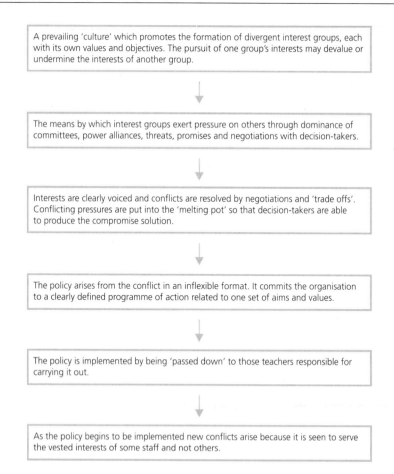

A prevailing 'culture' which promotes the formation of divergent interest groups, each with its own values and objectives. The pursuit of one group's interests may devalue or undermine the interests of another group.

The means by which interest groups exert pressure on others through dominance of committees, power alliances, threats, promises and negotiations with decision-takers.

Interests are clearly voiced and conflicts are resolved by negotiations and 'trade offs'. Conflicting pressures are put into the 'melting pot' so that decision-takers are able to produce the compromise solution.

The policy arises from the conflict in an inflexible format. It commits the organisation to a clearly defined programme of action related to one set of aims and values.

The policy is implemented by being 'passed down' to those teachers responsible for carrying it out.

As the policy begins to be implemented new conflicts arise because it is seen to serve the vested interests of some staff and not others.

The second example of organisational structure is the *collegial model*. Many primary schools display features of this model and some secondary schools view it as a state of nirvana well worth working towards. Indeed, this model has become the watchword of good practice in the management of schools, and inspectors, for example, see it as the key ingredient in school improvement and effectiveness. Collegial models are based on the notion of power sharing leading to discussion and consensus-based decision making. Teachers are encouraged to share knowledge and expertise and to work together in groups towards the mutually agreed aims of the school. The chief characteristics of collegial schools can be summarised like this:

- equal value is attached to both subject expertise and collaboration amongst teachers;

- 'task' or 'working' groups report back their recommendations for development and change to meetings of the whole staff;

- groups are led by subject coordinators or other significant postholders (such as SENCOs!) who marshal expertise from outside as well as inside the school so that curriculum development is based on a synthesis of authoritative opinion;

- the headteacher is the 'supporter' or 'enabler' who has consciously delegated responsibility for decision making to the whole staff;

- they are based on idealistic principles of democratic participation and 'management by agreement';

- authority is seen to derive from professional knowledge and expertise rather than from hierarchical position and this authority is harnessed to ensure coherent approaches to teaching and learning;

- values and educational objectives are shared and harmonised in all managerial activities so as to deny the existence of conflict;

- in large schools there is a formal committee system in which all sub-sections of the school are represented but not necessarily by subject leaders;

- the search for consensus and agreement is often time consuming and prolongs the process of policy making, but this is seen as a price worth paying for a conflict-free ethos.

Schools displaying the characteristics of the collegial model are likely to approach policy making in the fashion illustrated by Fig. 5.3.

FIG. 5.3 Policy making in 'collegial' institutions

All staff subscribe to whole school aims. Policy issue arises from desire to accomplish aims in a 'better' way.

Issue is discussed in different parts of the organisation and policy proposals are agreed based on 'expert' perspectives.

A 'task group' is formed and meets as often and for as long as necessary until agreement is reached on the main policy proposals and objectives.

Proposals are brought before the whole staff for discussion. Task group meets to discuss amendments and to re-state the objectives of the policy.

Full draft of the policy is discussed by whole staff. Staff meet for as long as is necessary to reach agreement.

Agreed policy is ratified by senior managers and governors and implemented according to agreed timescales.

Original task group continues to meet as a policy monitoring group and to provide expert professional guidance.

The purpose of this brief examination of two of the possible six organisational models in schools is to show the *context* within and against which SENCOs must work in order to manage change through policy development. Each organisational model has merits and although the collegial model gives teachers a greater sense of ownership of the policies they have helped to develop, the truth is that in many schools the headteacher is reluctant to relinquish the ultimate power of veto. Also, there is a form of 'pseudo-collegialism' where the impetus for policy development comes from senior managers and 'consultation' is substituted for participation. Policies come gift-wrapped and labelled 'fully discussed' or 'ratified by a whole staff meeting' as if this qualifies for collegiality. What is more, conflict in an organisation is not necessarily a 'bad thing'. Personality clashes apart, genuine disagreements over teaching or curriculum matters could be viewed as a sign of 'organisational health' leading to professional debate and a widening rather than a narrowing approach to learning.

TASK 23

Determining the model

Two models of school organisation have been described. Which model best fits a description of your school?

You have been asked to produce a policy for the education of gifted and talented children. Plot the path that the policy will take using either of the two models.

The SENCO as policy maker

How, then, should SENCOs approach policy making, especially with regard to developing a policy for educating gifted and talented pupils? To some degree this depends on whether the SENCO's role in the school is that of leader-manager or participant-manager. *Leader-managers* see their prime function as that of managing change through other people: they act as the catalyst for change, suggest solutions and support the process through advice and professional expertise. *Participant-managers* see their role as being responsive to the demands of others, including pupils and parents, and their prime function is to translate ideas into practical reality. This is similar to the idea of 'discoverers' or 'settlers' referred to in Chapter 1. Second, there is the concept of authority. If the SENCO has been asked to produce a policy, upon whose authority is the policy to be based? The headteacher and governors? Other management colleagues? The SENCO him/herself? The answer is critical if the 'gap' between policy and practice referred to on page 100 is to be as narrow as possible. *Authority* is a product of power and influence. Power has its origins in status, influence derives from professional knowledge and expertise. In other words, is the headteacher expecting the policy to be successful because of the status of those who have produced it or because of the level of professional expertise brought to bear? Or, does the SENCO carry sufficient authority in the school to be the initiator of the policy, thus reducing the headteacher's role to that of participant-manager? Third, there is the question of *opportunism*, the 'why me?' factor. Colleagues responsible for subjects or curriculum areas have a major responsibility for how teachers teach and how pupils respond to those specific areas. Senior managers have a responsibility for curriculum structure, but who, apart from the SENCO, looks at how individual pupils react to the whole curriculum? The SENCO is already concerned with curriculum adaptation to meet individual needs and with dispensing advice across the whole curriculum, so who is better placed to deliver a policy for the most able?

Faced with the requirement to produce a policy for the very able in a school, SENCOs should follow the pattern suggested by Table 5.6.

TABLE 5.6 Producing a policy

- Definition of need. Proportion of pupils concerned. Identification procedures defined, use of data and checklists. Define problem in the most precise terms possible.

- Establish the pressure points. Does impetus come from pupils, parents, headteacher, other colleagues with vested interests? SENCOs need to establish exactly where the pressure for a policy comes from.

- Clarify the authority. Who needs the policy? Is it top down or bottom up? Extent of prior discussion/publicity? Policy based on expertise or status? Is SENCO leading or reacting?

- Assemble the team. Interest group or task team? Team based on expertise or status? Establish role of SENCO in leading the team or responding to its demands.

- Establish the timescales. How much time is allowed for deliberations? Who determines this? Is full consensus necessary or is there a need for compromise by a particular date?

- Identify the objectives. What are the precise changes proposed? Full discussion of implications necessary. What are the benefits to the whole school? Links with whole school aims?

- Establish the feedback process. Who needs to be consulted? How can the widest possible participation be achieved? What are the logistical arrangements for full staff meetings? Are there interim committees?

- Main proposals. Concentrate on broad issues. Detail will be subject to discussion and amendment. The first priority is to establish broad principles.

- Anticipate challenge. Once the whole staffroom is involved challenge is inevitable. Have answers ready by anticipating challenges. Be prepared to amend main proposals.

- Draft policy. Present draft policy to appropriate approving body explaining both need and objectives. Demonstrate cost-benefit by minimising extra resources and maximising pupil outcomes.

- Produce policy. Follow model structure suggested. Avoid extensive change to daily practices. Spell out monitoring procedures and monitoring responsibility clearly. Reiterate school aims.

_____ IEPs and effective communication _____

In fulfilling the role of coordinating provision across the whole curriculum, SENCOs must acknowledge that it is virtually impossible to know what is happening inside every classroom all of the time. Some monitoring procedures involving classroom observations or feedback from support staff can be very effective, but there is one instrument which can achieve both a management function and ensure that pupils with SEN are given the correct attention – the Individual Education Plan. From the curriculum standpoint the IEP can focus very specifically on the educational needs of individual pupils and some schools have extended the principle to include the setting of targets to improve behaviour through an Individual Behaviour Plan (IBP) or to concentrate care and guidance on vulnerable pupils by using a Pastoral Support Plan. In each case the *management* functions are the same: negotiation, planning, communication, monitoring and concentrating resources on accomplishing a narrowly defined objective. There is also a further aspect of effective management which is often neglected by middle management postholders in schools: ensuring that planning takes account of other policies in operation.

TASK 24

Integration of policies

The majority of IEPs are literacy based, examine two such IEPs at random.

Highlight those features of the IEP which are directly related to the school's literacy policy.

How could you improve the design of the IEP to incorporate relevant aspects of the school's policies and approaches to literacy and numeracy?

What features of the Literacy Hour in particular could be 'built in' to the IEP?

It is not the intention of this short section of the chapter to discuss the detail of the contents and format of an IEP. It is interesting to note, however, that in many schools there is as much attention paid to how IEPs are written and presented as to their prime function. In many ways this is understandable in the search for a coherent and universally acceptable approach and it does at least demonstrate the essential feature of teachers working together in order to get something right. Please refer to Table 5.7 on page 108 for the characteristics of IEPs recommended by the Code of Practice and to Table 5.8 on page 108 for additional features suggested by a survey ('The Code of Practice: three years on' (1999)) of the use of IEPs in schools.

TABLE 5.7 Essential characteristics of IEPs

The concept of an IEP is first introduced in the SEN Code of Practice in connection with the placement of a child at either Stage 2 or Stage 3. It suggests that the SENCO should ensure that an IEP is drawn up. The essential characteristics of an IEP identified in the Code of Practice are that:

- it should focus on the specific learning difficulties of the child;
- it should take account of what the child has already achieved, building on the curriculum the child is following;
- there should be clear targets to be achieved over a specific period of time;
- both the child, and where possible the parents, should be involved in its preparation and review;
- at Stage 3, the advice of outside specialists should be sought.

TABLE 5.8 Additional recommendations

The findings of the survey carried out by the office of Her Majesty's Chief Inspector of Schools suggested that IEPs should:

- be seen as working documents;
- use a simple format;
- specify only provision and targets which are extra and additional to those generally available for, or expected to be achieved by, all pupils;
- avoid jargon;
- be comprehensible to all staff and parents;
- be distributed to all staff as necessary;
- promote effective planning by teachers;
- help pupils understand what progress they are making;
- link assessments of the progress of all pupils, including those with special educational needs, to the school;
- result in sound preparation and action by the staff, and the achievement of specific learning goals for the pupil.

One major factor which SENCOs need to be aware of in creating systems for planning IEPs is that the involvement of 'outside specialists' at Stage 3 has not happened in the way originally envisaged by the Code of Practice. In many LEAs the help given where pupils have visual or auditory impairment is usually adequate but resources do not often stretch to cover assessment and monitoring of pupils with other difficulties. Help with IEP reviews is also rare. The implications of this are that SENCOs need to quickly acquire a wide range of specialist knowledge and ensure that the IEP is an accurate vehicle for transmitting that knowledge to others.

The purpose of IEPs

If IEPs are to be effective in pinpointing the nature of children's special needs then the process requires systematic management. To begin with, the SENCO needs to establish the *main purposes* of the plans. Given that the principal function of a manager is to accomplish objectives through other people, it is essential that colleagues are always aware of the reasons for actions. Additionally, IEPs stand a better chance of being accepted as fundamental to a teacher's planning if there has been an element of participation in their creation. The central purpose of an IEP, of course, is to *communicate* essential information to colleagues about individual pupils:

■ the targets which the pupil should aim to meet;

■ the resources and strategies which should be used;

■ timescales; and

■ procedures for monitoring and review.

However, there are six further secondary purposes which are valuable assets in enabling SENCOs to become effective managers. IEPs can:

■ contribute to a coherent system for managing targets for all pupils across the curriculum;

■ enable SENCOs to bring together teachers from all disciplines so that the educational issues surrounding the teaching of skills can be thoroughly aired under expert leadership;

■ inculcate a wider sense of responsibility for special needs throughout the school;

■ be used to formalise links between key stages;

■ be used as a means of managing professional inputs from external agencies; and

■ promote a more meaningful approach to development planning based on improvements to teaching and learning.

Figure 5.4 on page 111 shows the range of positive advantages which can result from effective use of IEPs, and the two short case studies which follow also illustrate some of these points. However, newly appointed SENCOs should be aware of how some LEAs have created a condition whereby IEPs are misused and this should be resisted wherever possible. Some LEAs include IEPs in determining funding arrangements for SEN because they believe IEPs provide access to quick and objective data. This does nothing to enhance the quality of IEPs because it places too much emphasis on the bureaucracy of categorising pupils and causes IEPs to be written to coincide with a funding timetable rather than as working documents to help assessment, planning and teaching.

CASE STUDY

Secondary school, Leeds

At this school there was a regular programme of termly workshops advertised to all staff to ensure they were aware of, and completed, their responsibilities to pupils with special educational needs. Their work in writing IEPs was written into their job descriptions and was taken into consideration during appraisal.

CASE STUDY

Primary school, West Midlands

The SENCO at this school, where there is also a sixty-place nursery, a resource base for ten pupils with moderate learning difficulties and a twenty-place pre-school assessment unit, had become very skilful in learning how to incorporate in Stage 3 IEPs the contributions from numerous external professionals.

The school received contributions from support teachers for hearing and visually impaired children, the educational psychologist specialising in pre-school assessment and the very detailed reports from the LEA's coordinator for speech and language.

The SENCO brings these all together, ensures that staff and parents are informed and also that the IEPs are reviewed.

The IEP was the link between all the different and essential contributions that assist the assessment and teaching of the pupils with special educational needs.

With fifty-one extensive IEPs in the school and four in the unit it was a major task to update and review each term. The SENCO chooses to use her time to produce and review the IEPs alongside the teacher because of the need to relieve hard-pressed teachers with large classes and numerous curriculum and administrative responsibilities.

FIG. 5.4 Positive advantages of IEPs

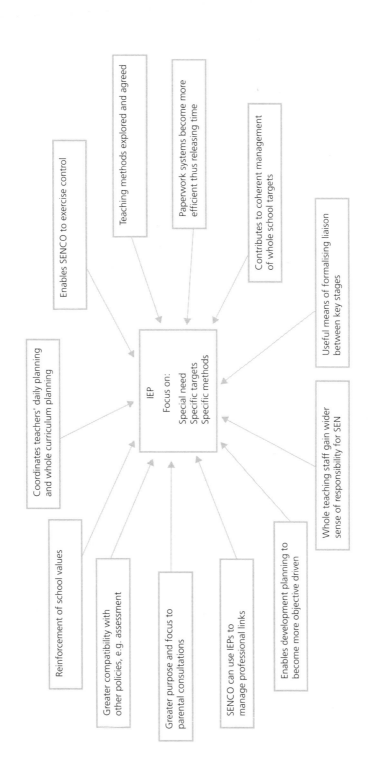

Enables SENCO to exercise control

Teaching methods explored and agreed

Paperwork systems become more efficient thus releasing time

Contributes to coherent management of whole school targets

Coordinates teachers' daily planning and whole curriculum planning

Reinforcement of school values

Greater compatibility with other policies, e.g. assessment

Greater purpose and focus to parental consultations

SENCO can use IEPs to manage professional links

Enables development planning to become more objective driven

IEP
Focus on:
Special need
Specific targets
Specific methods

Useful means of formalising liaison between key stages

Whole teaching staff gain wider sense of responsibility for SEN

Managing the IEP process

Having established that the IEP is both a means of identifying short-term corrective strategies for individual pupils and a useful vehicle for many of the management responsibilities held by SENCOs, newly appointed postholders will find it valuable to follow this guidance in managing the IEP process.

■ Most SENCOs are not concerned with the broad areas of whole school strategic management except as 'participating managers'. Time is often very limited so there needs to be one major aspect of implementing both the Code of Practice and the school's own policy which brings together significant aspects of management. The IEP enables the SENCO to show *leadership* through meetings with teachers, either individually or in groups, which have a specific focus on curriculum adaptation and teaching strategy. There is also the opportunity to establish the *authority* which comes from expert knowledge and which can permeate the whole curriculum. Additionally, the IEP process can be used to enhance the means by which support staff are managed because it provides a very clear direction to their work and draws them into a *team* approach to working with subject or class teachers.

■ IEPs can be used to provide the focus for additional support and advice from outside the school. One of the SENCO's major responsibilities is to ensure that practical guidance is available from external agencies and a prime function of all effective management is the coordination of sources of expertise – achieving objectives through other people. SENCOs need to take advantage of the fact that LEAs should have a vested interest in contributing to Stage 3 IEPs because this could result in significant reductions in the numbers of pupils at Stages 4 and 5 with the consequent availability of more specialised resources in areas of greatest need. External support is most effectively managed where it is specifically channelled towards assisting teachers in devising clear and measurable learning targets.

■ The most productive approach in a *secondary school* is to set up a working group with representation from each subject area. Devolving responsibility to heads of departments usually results in IEPs becoming relegated to the status of a 'low-level' issue. Better to give proper attention to an interest group through which a better understanding of SEN issues can be achieved. If the formulation of IEPs becomes a principal function of the group the SEN manager will be able to achieve the twin objectives of curriculum coherence and a common approach to the teaching of basic skills.

■ In a *primary school* the most effective approach is one which releases sufficient time for teachers to write IEPs. In this respect SENCOs need to work closely with senior management to devise regular opportunities for teachers to meet and work together. In most primary schools IEPs are the result of discussions between teachers and parents prior to children being placed on the register. The management role of the SENCO is therefore one of creating the opportunities for discussions to take place. Assembly and story time can be used to release teachers regularly each week, or the example of one school in Herefordshire can be followed where there is always one staff meeting per term for staff to write IEPs together, with the SENCO acting as a consultant. Managers must always be concerned with creating the conditions whereby objectives are successfully accomplished, and these two short case studies illustrate how two experienced SENCOs approached their management role.

CASE STUDY

Primary school, Yorkshire

IEPs for Stages 1–5 were completed termly. Targets were well written and formed short-term objectives that could be clearly evaluated at the next review or earlier if necessary.

The IEP contained only one aim, which was broken down into two or three targets within the aim.

The SENCO met each teacher once a term for half a day to talk about all the children on the register, evaluate results, and agree and write new targets. In addition there were informal meetings and reviews. Bilingual staff were involved in helping parents and teachers review progress. Targets were kept to a minimum and reflected their priority. Most pupils had only one target, but pupils at Stages 3 and 5 could have three.

The IEPs did not work in isolation. They were supported by a strong and effective behaviour policy, a social training programme and a school funded two-week holiday reading programme.

CASE STUDY

Primary school, West Midlands

This school had produced school guidelines for all staff to use when writing their IEPs. The school used more than one IEP format but all had shared criteria such as 'target date', 'who monitors', etc. Choice depended on suitability for the child. Target dates could also vary, for example, some needed to be set half-termly or even weekly. Sensible advice was given about setting realistic targets and the audience for IEPs. The SENCO was a full-time teacher with only a small amount of non-contact time every fortnight. She was able to offer suggestions and coordinate but all IEPs at both stages were the responsibility of teachers. The teachers incorporated advice from external agencies (if it had been provided) and they contacted and undertook a review with parents. They also had the use of classroom support.

What these two case studies clearly show, in management terms, is the importance of making the best use of limited time in a planned way, how objectives can be met by working with and empowering others, and how a guidance framework can be used to achieve coherence without compromising the professional judgement of colleagues.

■ In all schools, any delegation of responsibility for producing IEPs must be accompanied by regular injections of staff development. All managers have a duty to either impart specialist knowledge or make arrangements for that knowledge to be acquired from other sources. SENCOs should be mindful of their role as the expert leader and the IEP is the ideal vehicle for encouraging colleagues to look critically at how children learn and to explore a range of teaching strategies. It is worth remembering that in management terms delegating responsibility is more professionally rewarding than delegating tasks, but for delegating responsibility to be truly effective, SENCOs should also delegate knowledge.

■ Finally, it is important to see management as essentially an integration activity. Successful managers, including SENCOs, see an important aspect of their role as that of 'keeping one eye on the big picture'. This has already been alluded to in Task 24 on page 107, but in relation to the management processes. In relation to IEPs, SENCOs should keep this maxim firmly in mind: 'Never manage anything in a vacuum.' SENCOs should see themselves as the catalyst for change using IEPs as the blunt instrument. Schools which already have sound systems for all aspects of planning and where teachers regularly set targets and review progress are more likely to have a positive attitude towards incorporating IEPs into the normal planning process. An example of the integrationist approach to management is shown by the following short case study.

Comprehensive school, East Midlands

This school had an SEN liaison group which met every half-term (the dates of which were entered on the school's calendar). The group was made up of a representative of each curriculum area and one of its purposes was to be the main communication link between the SENCO and all curriculum areas.

The SENCO attended all curriculum team and pastoral team meetings as well as the school's strategy group, INSET committee and language working group. Details were fed back to the learning support department meetings, which took place every two weeks for one hour.

All team members attended the SEN liaison group meetings. The group had an identified aim and specific objectives which included exploring teaching strategies and developing each curriculum area's response to the SEN Code of Practice.

This section of the chapter has taken one aspect of a SENCO's responsibility and linked it to a number of management functions. For newly appointed SENCOs IEPs represent an ideal mechanism for bringing together the skills of team building, planning, keeping a focus on teaching and learning objectives, and influencing curriculum change.

TASK 25

Refining the IEP process

Consider how IEPs are written and acted upon in your school.

How can the management of IEPs be improved in order to create a greater sense of corporate responsibility for pupils with SEN?

Discuss with colleague SENCOs in other schools how LEA specialist support for Stage 3 IEPs can be improved.

All case study material in this section is taken from 'The SEN Code of Practice: three years on', a report from the office of Her Majesty's Chief Inspector of Schools (1999), published by OFSTED. All material is reproduced here with the permission of the Controller of Her Majesty's Stationery Office.

——————— Management tasks and ——————— the SENCO role

The 1994 Code of Practice originally envisaged that the SENCO role would encompass the traditional areas of teaching children with special educational needs and coordinating provision across the whole curriculum. The list of responsibilities is given in full in Chapter 2 on page 18. Within that list of tasks are aspects which are purely administrative in nature, such as maintaining the register, and which do not really fit any acceptable definition of management. However, there are other responsibilities which involve influencing the work of colleagues, establishing policy, contributing to planning and showing expert leadership, which are most definitely management functions.

The Code of Practice cites seven key areas of responsibility for SENCOs which intertwine two distinct aspects of the post:

1 responsibility for pupils at the individual level;

2 responsibility for policy enactment at the whole school level.

Each SENCO has to reconcile both elements into a coherent whole. Although there is considerable overlap between the two areas, it is clear that four of the key responsibilities are aimed primarily at some form of relatively short-term 'corrective' intervention on behalf of pupils who are not coping with the curriculum as it stands. The other three are mainly concerned with developmental issues such as training and working effectively with a variety of colleagues from other disciplines.

Other chapters of this book have examined the important management functions associated with implementing the school's SEN policy, and earlier sections of this chapter have looked at team building and approaches to policy making. It is important, therefore, that this chapter on management methodology concludes by looking at the implications behind the SENCO's role in development planning, coordinating the activities of support staff and overseeing the multi-disciplinary approach to pupils with statements. Other, more general, aspects of management such as how to manage change and professional development, together with further considerations of curriculum management, are of more concern to SENCOs as they become established in the role: refer to the Tailpiece, see 'Moving forward in the role', page 201.

Development planning provides an opportunity for SENCOs to be involved at three different levels:

 as the leader of the SEN 'team' responsible for devising and implementing the SEN development plan;

2 as the authoritative 'expert' advising subject leaders on the SEN element of curriculum area development plans; and

3 as the 'advocate' for change, development, training and resources to be included in the school development plan.

The degree to which all, some or none of these levels apply depends entirely on the extent to which the headteacher has delegated functional management responsibility to the SENCO. For instance, the 'advocacy' role can only be accomplished if the SENCO has sound knowledge of the structure of the school's finances and is privy to detailed discussions about whole school developmental priorities. Similarly, a culture of participation and collaborative teamwork will be far more receptive to the SENCO's advice on the SEN content of subject development plans. An organisational structure based on a hierarchy of status which places the SENCO way down the pecking order is less likely to be as receptive. It is a question of authority and acceptability, for there is no doubt that in terms of influencing development planning, the SENCO is a powerful agent for change. Planning is the process by which change is enacted, so in that sense *all* planning is development planning.

All the literature which examines the processes involved in development planning stresses the common features of observed best practice. Writing in *Education Management in Action* (eds Crawford, Kydd and Parker (1994)) the deputy head of a secondary school underlines the importance of the school development plan as the means of enacting change. However, the plan itself will achieve nothing unless it is seen to be part of a systematic process of setting and reviewing objectives involving the whole staff's awareness of the short-term goals of the school. This exemplifies a common theme found in the literature: the need to distinguish between the desired outcomes and the means of accomplishing them. Early studies on school improvement showed the importance of staff development in improving overall teaching and learning so that many schools adopted the paradigm 'there is no curriculum development without staff development and vice versa' as the overriding approach to development planning. Studies in the early part of the 1990s all pointed to the importance of establishing a close correlation between whole school development, staff development and developments in daily classroom practice. The conclusion drawn by an extensive study into the role of development planning in improving school effectiveness conducted by MacGilchrist and others (1995) was that only one type of plan was successful in bringing about these tripartite improvements. The three principles behind the successful plan should be borne in mind by all SENCOs, and all school managers for that matter, and these are:

- the plan is well led and managed;

- the professional development of teachers is a constant factor;

- the central focus of the plan is on pupils' achievements and progress.

The leadership and management of the plan is crucially important. Hargreaves and Hopkins (1991) show that establishing a plan is one thing, making sure the plan is actually implemented is another. The best plans are those which can be easily managed; the need for over-management is the sign of a poor plan. The danger lies in assuming that a plan will manage itself, so it is important to identify the key figures who will be responsible for carrying the plan forward and for monitoring its effectiveness. Nor should leadership and management be confined to those occupying status-based roles in the hierarchy. This leads to a feeling of exclusion on the part of many teachers and the tendency to rely on 'managers' for ideas and innovation.

Staff development does not just relate to topic-specific items in the development plan; giving teachers an opportunity to develop as practitioners through a leadership or monitoring role identified in the plan is just as legitimate and valuable. The chances are, however, that the SENCO will assume responsibility for leading and managing most aspects of an SEN development plan and it is useful to apply the same definitions to leadership and management as to effectiveness and efficiency:

Leadership (effectiveness) = doing the right things

Management (efficiency) = doing things in the right way.

TASK 26

Analysing leadership and management in planning

Identify an objective in a previous school, subject or SEN development plan which was particularly successfully accomplished.

What are the most notable features of the way the objective is expressed?

How is the objective directly linked to pupils' achievements and progress?

What practical examples of good leadership and management contributed to the success of this part of the plan?

In development planning terms, leadership, or doing the right things, means identifying the correct priorities and expressing them in clear objectives. The importance of making objectives explicit and unambiguous cannot be overstressed. There are a number of good reasons for this, not least of which is the fact that so many subject development plans appear as little more than 'wish lists'. SENCOs need to distinguish between a *wish*, an *aim* and an *objective*. This explanation will help:

'Everybody knowing what is going on'	=	a wish
'Developing a better communication system'	=	an aim
'Producing a fortnightly newsletter'	=	an objective

CASE STUDY

'The Magic Carpet'

An item in a subject development plan had 'A new carpet in Room 3' as an objective. The intended outcome of this was to be a quieter and more studious atmosphere, less litter and a greater respect for materials and furniture. This appeared on each development plan for three years, the carpet never materialised, and the item did not appear on the plan in year four. Why?

In year five a newly appointed subject coordinator had as a central aim the improvement of pupils' attitudes towards the subject and the first objective was 'to increase the numbers of pupils opting for the subject by improving the environment for learning'. Amongst the strategies for achieving this was a detailed analysis of how different floor coverings reduced noise levels (the subject was music) and a costed recommendation. Room 3 had its carpet five weeks later. Why?

As with most aspects of management, a systematic approach to development planning works best. (For a complete step-by-step practical guide to development planning see *Middle Management in Schools Manual*, Shuttleworth (2000).) The section on team building at the beginning of this chapter emphasises the importance of widening the circle of participants in the process. This is particularly important if the means of accomplishing objectives depend upon the cooperation of colleagues across the curriculum and if the objectives are 'correct', that is linked to improved teaching and learning. A good way to involve others in the process is to view development planning as a cycle of activity rather than as a 'one-off' because the headteacher wants all the plans by a certain date. As Fig. 5.5 below shows, the planning cycle begins with an evaluation of the previous plan and this should involve all teachers and support staff who were involved in its implementation. This brings all staff together in a 'team' approach.

FIG. 5.5 The planning cycle

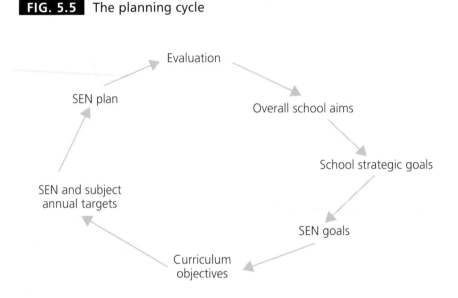

The advantage of this process cycle view is that it enables planning to have a very sharp focus at key critical points. For example, all development plans should have regard for the advancement of overall school aims; and how those aims are translated into short-term school strategic goals provides the framework for planning. This helps to create the sort of unified corporate plan seen to be the most successful by MacGilchrist and others (1997). This approach also enables the SENCO to be the planner, advisor and advocate referred to at the beginning of this section. Table 5.9 on page 122 gives a starting point by providing a suggested template for a team evaluation of the previous plan.

Developing a plan

The actual format for presenting development plans varies considerably between schools, and the method of presentation often says much about the 'sharpness' of focus on teaching and learning objectives. Whatever the method, efficient management is both demonstrated and facilitated by following these six principles.

1 SENCOs should resist the temptation to advance on too broad a front. Development planning implies change and to be effective the quantity of change should be minimised in favour of quality. Three or four broad aims should be sufficient, two of which are contributory aims to whole school development and one or two very specific to SEN aims, linked to the advancement of the school's SEN policy.

2 Each aim should be qualified by a series of objectives. These need to be worded very specifically in terms of improvements to teaching and learning. The outcomes of these objectives should always be a demonstrable increase in standards of achievement and rates of progress.

3 The focus should be on the means as well as the ends. Here, the simplest technique to use in team discussions is to always link 'to' and 'by'. Our objective is '*to* achieve A' and we are going to do this '*by* methods B, C and D'. This links forward to Chapter 6: 'Setting targets to raise the standards of pupils' achievements' where every pupil *outcome* target is automatically linked to a school *process* target.

4 For SENCOs, the overall theme of development planning must be the management of the curriculum. The plan should spell out how provision across the whole curriculum is to be enhanced, and with what anticipated results. This should provide the focus for the development of areas such as differentiation, teaching strategies and the means by which teachers' knowledge and expertise are to be increased.

5 Plans need to be as specific as possible about timescales, resources and implications for costs. Plans are not abstract meanderings devoid of reality, they are working documents firmly linked to spending priorities and teachers' daily classroom practice.

6 Finally, successful implementation comes from ownership. All colleagues, including support staff, must feel that they have a contribution to make. The most successful SEN development plans clearly state the specific roles of individuals in overseeing, monitoring or actually implementing aspects of the plan.

TASK 27

Development planning

In a meeting of the SEN 'team', focus attention on an area of development that all team members agree is necessary.

Define the anticipated outcomes in terms of how pupils' achievements and progress will improve.

Frame the objective in specific and clear language, beginning with the word 'to....'.

Identify the strategies, resources, personnel and training needs by using the word 'by....'.

TABLE 5.9 Measuring success

Assess last year's development plan against the following criteria by assigning a score in the boxes.

HIGH 1 2 3 4 5 LOW

- Impact on the management and organisation of the department ☐
- Impact on the professional development of teachers ☐
- Impact on pupils' learning in the classroom ☐
- Impact on beliefs and attitudes ☐
- Plan was well led and managed ☐
- Teacher development was built in ☐
- Focus was on targets for pupil attainment and progress ☐
- Changes to equipment and materials were indicated ☐
- Changes to classroom practices and teaching styles were indicated ☐
- Adjustments to the way pupils are grouped were proposed ☐
- The whole department was involved/teachers were stakeholders ☐
- Objectives were clear, precise and sharply focused ☐
- Expected learning outcomes were monitored and evaluated systematically ☐
- All targets were met, on time and within agreed budget levels ☐

Resource management

Coordinating the activities of support staff is an important function of personnel management which has implications for the role of all SENCOs in all schools. Numbers and types of support teachers or assistants may vary, but the SENCO's role remains the same. A distinction must be drawn between the kind of professional support provided by LEAs for pupils with statements or sensory impairment, and Learning Support Assistants (LSAs). Professional support is managed by the LEA according to its total resources and the relationships established with schools as a result of Local Management of Schools (LMS). Learning Support Assistants, also known in education management literature as paraprofessionals, are managed by the SENCO according to availability and need.

In respect of professional support the SENCO has the responsibility of working with the LEA to determine what level and type of expert assistance is necessary. To a large degree this is determined by three considerations:

1 specific needs of individual children for whom full access to the curriculum would be denied without 'expert' and narrowly focused help;

2 the role of LEA SEN support staff in preventative measures such as in-service training, advisory or consultative work so that the wider needs of all children are met through, for example, guidance on the development of a differentiated curriculum;

3 the extent to which LEA support services are 'named' in statements, especially in fulfilling the statutory duty to monitor and review the progress of pupils and the adherence to the terms of the statement.

In this regard the SENCO cannot, and should not, be expected to take full responsibility. It is here that the closeness of the working relationship with the headteacher is most important because the prevailing culture is one which sees the LEA as the *provider* of services and the school as the *purchaser* of those services. Only the headteacher has the authority to establish and act upon spending priorities. The SENCO's role, therefore, is one of coordinating management decisions taken elsewhere, but also one of recommending how priorities can be addressed, as this case study illustrates.

CASE STUDY

'Martine'

Martine is SENCO at a large 9–13 middle school in the Home Counties. After three years in the post she was not entirely dissatisfied with the level of service provided by the LEA but felt it was too 'ad hoc' and depended on both personal relationships and the speed with which the LEA could react to situations. She decided a more professional approach was called for. Following a series of meetings with other SENCOs in the area and LEA SEN management staff, a service level agreement was drawn up which resulted, for Martine's school, in:

- SEN support staff conducting both twilight and training day staff development sessions to support pupils at Stages 1 and 2;

- a programme of six visits by LEA staff to advise and work with the SENCO and subject staff on intervention strategies and the composition of IEPs at Stage 3.

When it comes to coordinating the work of other professionals, experienced SENCOs will invariably say that the personal quality they have had to develop is assertiveness in the face of conflicts of interest. LEA support staff are agents of the local authority, not of the school, and as such are controlled by central policy and budgetary considerations. Nowhere is this highlighted more sharply than in the SENCO's responsibility for coordinating the multi-disciplinary approach to statements. An educational psychologist, for example, could be placed in a position where independent judgement is compromised, as this case study illustrates.

CASE STUDY

'Maurice'

Maurice was a pupil at a small primary school in East Anglia. He had considerable learning difficulties which did not result in satisfactory progress at Stage 2. The educational psychologist was asked to support the school following the decision to place Maurice on Stage 3. After proper assessment an IEP was drawn up. The educational psychologist and the SENCO worked closely with the class teacher to produce supportive resources and to identify how the curriculum could be differentiated. Maurice's progress was monitored carefully. Over time both the class teacher and Maurice's parents felt that insufficient progress was being made and requested a statutory assessment. The psychologist, however, believed that the Stage 3 intervention strategy had not been in operation long enough for a proper judgement on progress. At this point the psychologist had to switch roles and offer his opinion on whether the Stage 4 criteria had been met. In effect the psychologist was now supporting the LEA and not Maurice. The school and Maurice's parents lost confidence in the so-called independent judgements.

The case study does not show failure on anybody's part, rather it highlights a potential danger to SENCOs who may seize upon any offer of professional assistance without thinking through the consequences.

Although LEAs must take responsibility for the provision of resources to support a statement, it is the SENCO who now has the pivotal role in liaising with other agencies. It is difficult to see this role strictly in management terms, rather it brings us back to the concept of coordinating provision. However, there are some functions of management which apply, namely:

■ concentrating resources on meeting specific objectives;

■ keeping the focus of attention on the main purpose of support – the needs of the child;

■ gathering and applying information;

■ calling, chairing and servicing meetings;

■ communicating decisions and disseminating educational programmes to colleagues;

■ harnessing the skills of disparate groups, such as teachers who typify the divide between education and care; and

■ developing models of good inter-agency practice through systematic evaluation of what is available.

By comparison, managing *paraprofessional* support is much more straightforward. Learning Support Assistants represent an increasing resource in our schools and it is widely acknowledged that they have a significant impact on the progress made by the children with whom they work. In many schools, however, neither their skills nor their time are managed effectively. There are some examples of excellent practice though, as these short case studies illustrate.

CASE STUDY

Mums who stayed

A primary school in North West England had one part-time teacher who had returned to the school after taking early retirement as its only source of classroom support. Four mothers came in during most mornings to help with 'slow readers'. The SENCO persuaded the headteacher to terminate the contract of the part-time teacher because the 'mum's army' wanted to spend more time in the school. Each of the mothers obtained the City and Guilds Certificate in Learning Support and adjusted their attendance times to provide a continuing programme of support in every class. One assistant has applied to become a full-time teacher at another school through the Graduate and Registered Teacher Programme. The school has a good level of support and value for money.

CASE STUDY

Observation and research

An experienced SENCO in a large secondary school in South London calls the LSAs 'my eyes and ears'. Nearly twenty per cent of all lessons are supported by LSAs who work closely with teaching staff on such matters as assessment and time given over to reflecting on teaching methods. The SENCO organises the LSAs into small project teams which carry out action research projects into methods of differentiation in different subjects.

What both these case studies show is the application of three essential management principles in regard to non-teaching staff:

- valuing staff for the contribution they make;

- extending the formal role beyond the minimum; and

- adopting a positive and proactive approach to inclusion and participation.

The latter principle is well illustrated in the earlier sections of this chapter on team building and the use of IEPs as a management tool. Similarly the section on development planning stresses the need for a quality input from the whole SEN team, including support staff.

It is essential that newly appointed SENCOs rapidly assimilate the needs and aspirations of support assistants so that other teaching colleagues can adopt equally positive attitudes.

TASK 28

Identifying needs

Arrange a meeting with Learning Support Assistants, this could be as a group or individually.

Ask each of them what the school could do to make their work more effective.

Ask each person to highlight their perception of their strengths and weaknesses.

Ask each person to say which pupils they like to work with most and least and why.

Draw up a needs-related training plan for each assistant.

It is equally important for SENCOs to understand how the role of the LSA has changed, especially since the introduction of the National Curriculum. Research shows that the role has undergone a subtle change in direct proportion to the influence of the SENCO over other teaching colleagues. In schools where the SENCO's influence on curriculum development is light, LSAs still have the *interpretative* role, that is adapting the content of lessons to match the needs of pupils, often with little prior knowledge of the purpose of the lesson. In schools where teachers have taken on responsibility for a differentiated curriculum for themselves, the expectation of LSAs is that they will help pupils to achieve target levels of achievement. Similarly, in schools where learning support is managed effectively other roles have been identified such as a concentration on areas of underachievement (like boys in certain subjects) or the implementation of strategies for improvements to behaviour.

When roles change, so do training needs. The fundamental precept behind such initiatives as 'Investors in People' and the prevailing attitude of our more enlightened colleagues in industry is 'if you develop the individual you will develop the organisation'. This immediately highlights the role of the SENCO as trainer and advisor. However, the demands of meeting targets in individual subjects become increasingly complex so the SENCO needs to enlist the help of other teaching colleagues in the training of LSAs.

In *management* terms, the three principles outlined earlier would be supplemented by the following actions to be undertaken by the SENCO:

- planned activities for training in subject-specific aspects;
- regular meetings to update the register and IEPs;
- meetings with subject staff to plan the content of lessons;
- discussion of the means of recording the nature of support and its effects on progress.

SENCOs need the support of LSAs to update the register and to keep IEPs current. If they are regarded as 'second class citizens' by the rest of the staff, these essential jobs will not get done.

———————— Summary ————————

■ Many aspects of a SENCO's role are purely administrative, but there are instances which call for the qualities of leadership and management. Effectiveness is not just a personal issue, it depends upon professional relationships, especially with the headteacher.

■ As in most areas of management the team approach works best. SENCOs are members of teams as well as leaders of their own team and so are well placed to observe team effectiveness. Teams work best when they are composed for a particular purpose and have the right blend of personalities. It is important to manage teams systematically and allow time for reflective evaluation of team performance. Leadership should seek to encourage active participation in accomplishing team goals. Teams should have very clear terms of reference and be more concerned with the task than with the status of their members. SENCOs need to train their teams in a systematic approach to meeting objectives.

■ SENCOs are well placed to advise schools on the structure and content of a policy for the education of gifted and talented children. Issues such as identification, assessment and specialist provision are common to giftedness and SEN. The approaches to policy making vary according to the nature of the school; 'political' schools will arrive at policies in a different way from 'collegial' organisations. It is the function of management to monitor the 'gap' between policy and practice. All policies should be based on a clearly defined need which is translated into workable objectives. Authority and ownership are vital components because the effectiveness of policies depends upon their 'worthwhileness' and the rigour of monitoring procedures.

■ Many facets of the SENCO's management role come together in the production of IEPs. The Code of Practice outlines the characteristics of IEPs and a recent HMI survey makes recommendations based on examples of good practice. The IEP is the ideal mechanism for communicating the SENCO's ideas across the whole curriculum and it is essential that there is a 'match' with other school policies and approaches to curriculum development. Apart from the vital function of pinpointing needs and provision for individual pupils, IEPs can be used as the vehicle for managing a coherent and multi-discipline approach to SEN. Case studies show how this is achieved in a variety of schools.

SENCOs must not only provide specialist advice, they must contribute towards systems which create adequate time for teachers to write IEPs.

- The list of responsibilities for SENCOs given in the Code of Practice is part administrative and part management. Some items focus on working with individual children and others imply a school-wide management role. Development planning gives a SENCO the opportunity to operate at three levels: planner, advisor and advocate. The best development plans distinguish between means and ends and forge a strong link between whole school, subject and professional development plans. The way a plan is led and managed is important. Leaders must give a clear set of priorities so that the team can concentrate on formulating objectives. Management is by participation and SENCOs can encourage this by a team evaluation of previous plans.

- The management of support staff is an important aspect of the SENCO's work. The level of service provided by an LEA should be placed on a formal footing and SENCOs can coordinate a variety of specialist inputs by keeping the focus on the needs of children rather than administrative processes. Communication and coordination are the two most important functions. Learning Support Assistants are vital to the progress made by pupils. They must be managed in a way which acknowledges their value, encourages full participation and takes account of their training needs in a developing role.

chapter six

Setting targets to raise the standards of pupils' achievements

Introduction

There is a statutory requirement placed upon all schools to set targets for the overall performance of pupils. The statutory regulations limit targeting pupils' achievements to English and mathematics at the end of Key Stage 2 and GCSE examinations at the end of Key Stage 4. However, all schools are encouraged to extend the process to include other subjects, other key stages and other priorities identified by the school or funding authority. The process of setting targets to raise the standards of pupils' achievements applies to *all* pupils in all maintained schools, including special schools. Pupils with special educational needs must be seen as part of this process for three main reasons:

- 'inclusion' means full participation in all measures adopted by a school to raise standards;

- targets are already the main ingredient of individual education plans; and

- there is scope for the setting of additional targets to include attitude, behaviour and teaching strategies.

SENCOs who are new to the position need guidance on how targets for pupils with SEN are determined, how such targets should form the main plank of development planning both at subject and whole school levels, and on the essential *management* functions needed to ensure that the right conditions for success are created. This chapter concentrates on these issues and further elaborates upon the management techniques encountered in previous chapters.

As more schools are beginning to gain experience in the processes of target setting some clear principles are emerging, and these should be noted by SENCOs who are embarking on this aspect of their work for the first time.

- Targets are defined as *forecasts* plus *challenge* so must be *realistic* and *achievable*. The only way that these criteria can be met is if the starting point – the *baseline* data and information – is both accurate and reliable.

- Many targets are expressed in terms of a percentage increase in measurable results of assessments by a whole school, year group or key stage. However, underpinning this is what happens at individual subject and class level which in turn becomes translated into how each child or pupil is to be encouraged to perform better. Setting targets for whole groups will not of itself produce better standards, this will only come about by the aggregation of many small steps.

- In selecting suitable measures of performance and appropriate timescales within which targets are expected to be met, most schools have chosen national standards expressed as National Curriculum levels and key stages. However, for pupils with SEN these may not be the most appropriate indicators so the use of other measures and timescales will be needed and SENCOs need to determine these. Where targets are dovetailed into the timescales for development planning, over one, two or even three years, targets for the progress of pupils with SEN have to be carefully planned to ensure they do not fall outside the timescales and hence run the real risk of being excluded from the development plan.

- It is essential that pupils are fully consulted and informed about their individual targets. They need to know why and how their performance should improve. This has implications for an additional workload on teachers, not only for planning teaching strategies based on the learning needs of all pupils but for the frequency with which pupils' progress is monitored through assessment and more thorough diagnostic marking. These implications are beginning to bite hard at teachers' energy levels and need sensitive management.

- Similarly, parents need to be kept much more informed about their child's targets so that progress can be reported at more frequent intervals. This has implications for record-keeping and the style of reports to parents. Many schools have had to give attention to refining their 'early warning system' so that *de facto* reporting of failure to achieve targets at the end of a twelve month period is avoided.

- Moreover, the dissemination of pupils' targets to all teachers across the curriculum is vital if pupils are to stand a realistic chance of accomplishing them. A specific literacy-related target is devalued if attention is paid to it on only a few occasions during the week when the pupil is doing English but ignored in written work in other subjects.

- There has to be the recognition that for each set of pupil *outcome* targets there will need to be a complementary set of *process* targets which figure prominently in all development plans. These express how the school intends to create the conditions within which pupils will be *enabled* to meet their targets. Resources and teaching methods are the prime candidates for process targeting.

- Finally, most schools have come to see the value of target setting as part of a holistic management process involving an evaluation of the school's performance against that of similar schools and an integrated approach to strategic planning, staff development and prioritising specific areas of work. Senior managers in schools which have successfully absorbed target setting into whole school management have also successfully involved the SENCO as a major team member.

There are many other messages deriving from the experiences of different schools and especially from the way assessment data is analysed as a predictor of future achievement either by the school or by a commercially available software package or by an external agency such as the National Foundation for Educational Research (NFER). However, the principal message that target setting is a complex process involving many facets of school life is one which SENCOs need to absorb before plunging in.

Essential management functions

When beginning the process of setting targets many schools have turned to their SENCO for advice – after all, pupils with special educational needs have been working towards targets for years. SENCOs have much to offer in this sphere by way of experience and they make a valuable contribution to the overall management of this aspect of school improvement. The setting of targets is not something which can be done piecemeal: there must be a systematic approach to planning and monitoring which operates to create a coherent whole out of something which operates at a number of different levels. On the one hand there is the need to set strategic goals at governor and headteacher level, and on the other there is a group of pupils, each one of whom must improve their performance. In between lies the whole question of how the appraisal of teachers can incorporate targets and a likely impact on very specifically focused professional development. For SENCOs there is the additional question of how best to engage their advisory role across the whole curriculum and the need to ensure that targets for pupils with SEN fall *inside* the school's overall strategy. Figure 6.1 expresses the levels, management aspects and links in a diagram.

FIG. 6.1 Management levels and functions in target setting

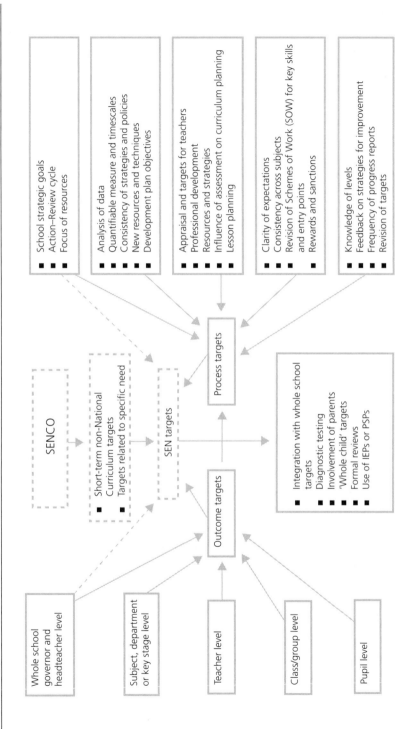

In terms of the SENCO's specific management functions there will be a wide variation across phases and between schools. However, there are five central features which should be common to most schools:

1 objective setting;

2 establishing the baseline;

3 pupil/parent focus;

4 curriculum liaison;

5 monitoring and recording progress.

Setting objectives

Objective setting is an essential first step because it involves defining the status quo and establishing the relationship between overall school targets and those for pupils with special needs. Whilst the overall aim is to raise the standards of all pupils, because targets are related to the proportions of pupils attaining levels or grades in national tests or examinations, it is inevitable that schools manage the process by redefining and narrowing the focus of their objectives. For example, some schools may seek to raise levels of attainment in certain subjects by focusing on monitoring teaching in those subjects or the provision of additional resources. Similarly, some schools may concentrate on the achievement of boys and prepare a range of strategies to tackle this common issue. Or, very commonly, there may be a focus on pupils deemed to be achieving at a level below the target level and these pupils are singled out for extra work, mentoring or specific attention in class. In other words, the aim is fulfilled by narrowing the objective. The SENCO needs to establish where and how targets for pupils with special needs fit into the school's objective focus. This is particularly important if the narrowing of the objective seems to exclude pupils with special needs. For instance, where an increase in the proportion of pupils attaining level 4 and above is to be achieved by concentrating on those pupils currently achieving level 3, what value is placed on pupils at levels 2, 1 or below in the school's management strategy? Of course, all teachers are concerned to ensure that *every* pupil is stretched to perform at the highest level of which they are capable, but this is not always apparent when targets are set which relate to national expectations of the 'average' and 'above average' child. The relationship to league tables and measures of school effectiveness is obvious, which is why SENCOs really need to force the issue of the 'value' placed on SEN targets.

One way of establishing and reinforcing this 'value' is through development planning. Development planning for SEN is covered more fully in Chapter 5: 'Methodology', but for the purposes of establishing 'value' in target setting these four principles should be noted.

■ The school development plan is a powerful document because it sends out clear messages about what the school has identified as its priorities and how it intends to accomplish them. The central focus should be on factors intended to bring about improvements to teaching and learning so all targets should feature prominently. It is essential that special educational needs is either given a separate section in the school plan or that there is the expectation that consideration is given to SEN in all sections. SENCOs must insist on this and headteachers have an obligation under the Code of Practice to ensure SEN is included in school development plans. This does not always happen.

■ Similarly, subject development plans should give due prominence to SEN issues as they impact upon future strategies. Too many subject plans do not give proper focus to teaching and learning so that objectives lack 'sharpness' and targets sometimes do not even rate a mention. Part of the SENCO's duty to coordinate provision across the curriculum is to ensure subject development plans reflect the development of teaching and learning for pupils with SEN.

■ Value is further enhanced if there is a separate development plan for special needs. Areas which should be particularly highlighted include resources for learning, curriculum modifications, teaching strategies and professional development (these make good headings). The simplest and most effective plans adopt the 'To ...... by ......' model (see Chapter 5: 'Methodology', page 121) because this leads to sharp objectives and a focus on method.

■ The whole planning process must be two way. Governors and senior managers must establish the priority areas and negotiate the improvement targets. Subject leaders and SENCOs then need to demonstrate how their targets and strategies will contribute to these. This is coordinated planning and avoids wasteful pages of 'wish lists' which never actually stand a chance of implementation.

TASK 29

Evaluating the school development plan

Examine the current whole school development plan.

Answer these questions.

1 Is there a separate section for SEN or is SEN prominent in all sections?

2 To what extent have subject plans and the SEN plan 'fed into' the school plan?

3 Are there clear priorities for improvements to teaching and learning, expressed as targets?

4 Which aspects of previous plans keep recurring? Why?

Establishing the baseline

Establishing the baseline is important in all target setting because pupils need to know the starting point. It is even more important for pupils with special needs because often the starting point is the careful analysis of the need itself. Teachers must also use the most appropriate resources and strategies if targets are to be met. This is where the aspect of management known as 'demonstrating professional knowledge and expertise' comes in, an aspect applicable to SENCOs more than to any other middle manager in a school. The main problem for SENCOs in relation to overall school targets is that pupils' needs do not fit neatly into the key stage system, so it is almost impossible to establish a baseline in a continuum of progress which is meaningful to subject teachers. Whatever the baseline, the most important management function is to communicate it to others. It is very likely that there will be a *range* of targets for pupils with SEN so awareness of this range and how it applies to different pupils must be communicated. IEPs are a useful vehicle for this because they individualise the targets, but a development plan cannot include each IEP so broader targets will have to be set. These broad targets will operate alongside specific pupil targets and will carry complementary process targets in the development plan. For example, the following aspects make good topics for targets:

- *time* – aiming to shorten the length of time it takes to accomplish something. This could be an aspect of pupils' progress or the completion of an administrative task;

- *frequency* – increasing or reducing how often something happens. Reporting to parents on progress may need frequency increasing, the frequency of classroom support for a particular pupil may be a target for reduction in line with improved progress;

- *proportion* – increasing or reducing the numbers of pupils for whom some form of special provision is made;

- *independence/intervention* – aiming to increase the opportunities for independent learning by reducing the frequency of intervention. Or, increasing the degree of earlier intervention could be a suitable target;

- *professional development* – the number of teachers being given specific training, a widening of the range of training opportunities or training linked to a specific pupil target.

In each case the management function is the same and has four strands:

- establish the baseline (for example, how many teachers have taken a Dyslexia Institute course?);

- set the target (*to* increase awareness of teaching strategies in relation to dyslexia);

- determine the methods (*by* arranging for five teachers to attend an Institute course by the end of the year);

- communicate to others.

TASK 30

Communicating targets to others

Establish a range of possible target topics similar to the ones given above.

For each topic establish who needs to know, in what detail, and at what stage (i.e. when target is set or met).

Establish the best means of communicating the nature and value of these targets.

Parental cooperation

Pupil/parent focus is a normal everyday aspect of the SENCO's role irrespective of targets. The need to involve, consult with and inform parents or other adults responsible for children's care and domestic arrangements is fundamental to the creed of the Code of Practice and is frequently highlighted throughout this book. It is also likely that some of the strategies for meeting targets will involve assistance at home and it is critical that parents and responsible adults understand the nature of the target and the reason for it. For example, a series of targets may be set for some pupils in the 'Personal and social development' category which may involve improvements to how pupils interact and work with others, say 'being better able to anticipate the consequences of actions and decisions'. To reinforce such targets it will be necessary to explain to parents what is not happening at present and what they must do to assist the child. A procedure for communication must be established, involving both meetings, letters, examples of how progress can be encouraged and reported, and a clear description of how the partnership with teachers will work, possibly involving other agencies such as social services.

Moreover, it may well be that there are weaknesses in the present system of involving parents. This could be the result of structural deficiencies in the way the SENCO's time is organised or a problem with neglect or apathy on the part of some parents. Whatever the problem, this could be the topic of another target so that not only are parents seen to be vital in helping to meet targets, their involvement is *ipso facto* a target in itself!

TASK 31

Establishing parental targets

Frame a target linked to the involvement of parents.

Discuss a range of options with the headteacher which will lead to meeting this target.

CASE STUDY

'Catherine'

Catherine is a SENCO in a medium-sized junior and infant school in the East Midlands. A teacher for over twenty years, most spent in her present school, Catherine became SENCO at the time the Code of Practice was introduced. She is a popular and much respected teacher to whom other SENCOs in the area often turn for advice.

At the end of the Spring term last year there were four pupils at Stage 2 who were giving Catherine real cause for concern and she needed to move them on to Stage 3, but not before she had spoken to their parents. This was her dilemma – these particular parents simply could not or would not respond to invitations to come to the school and ignored her suggestions that she visit them at home. Relationships with all other parents were excellent so Catherine knew the problem was an isolated one.

Catherine decided that she needed a strategy to deal with this problem now and also a target to ensure a similar problem would not arise in future because it was delaying an essential step in the educational provision for the children.

■ Frame a suitable target for Catherine and discuss a range of strategies which may be successful in establishing parental contact.

Catherine was eventually successful in meeting these parents, some of whom had other problems related to unemployment, long working hours and complete misunderstanding of the system. She involved the headteacher, social services, employers, friends and neighbours and parents of other children. Her most successful strategy was a 'surgery' from 5–6 pm on Monday evenings held away from the school at a local community centre.

Involving parents in target setting and target meeting is not something which can happen instantly. Some parents will be apprehensive about their role, some will have had bad experiences of the education system, some will be too eager to push the child too hard and others will adopt the view that education 'is the school's job'. SENCOs must manage each situation with sensitivity and patience and, above all, coordinate the involvement of colleagues and other agencies so that approaches are consistent and based on trust.

Once parental trust and involvement is secure, as it will be in the majority of cases, a meeting should be fixed at the earliest possible opportunity. Many schools have used the 'normal' programme of meetings with parents to explain overall targets and there are several variations of the 'home-school agreement' into which targets can be fitted. Others have used the annual progress reports to include an extra sheet explaining what parents can do to help. For experienced SENCOs the involvement of parents in the target setting process is simply an extension of everyday good practice.

Communication with colleagues

Curriculum liaison is another characteristic role which applies to target setting. Two aspects of management apply here:

■ involving teachers in the setting of targets;

■ communicating targets to all teachers;

and SENCOs need to devise procedures for these. In a secondary school this will involve discussions with subject teachers on the most appropriate subject-specific targets and how these can be incorporated into IEPs, for example; or alternatively, subject teachers need to be shown how aspects of learning in that subject can contribute towards meeting more general literacy, numeracy or personal development targets. In primary schools there will be an extra reliance on each class teacher's knowledge of the children concerned and some kind of formal agreement between the class teacher and the SENCO on the precise details of targets and how progress will be monitored. In all schools each set of targets must be accompanied by advice on resources, teaching strategies and how and when to judge progress. SENCOs need to establish clear and consistent procedures for how targets permeate the curriculum.

TASK 32

Managing targets across the curriculum

Devise and establish procedures for the following:

- negotiating targets with subject or class teachers;
- recording advice given on resources and teaching methods;
- assessment and recording of progress.

Is the IEP a suitable vehicle for this or will another simple proforma need designing?

Evaluating the results

Monitoring and recording progress are essential if target setting is to have any effect. SENCOs need to be absolutely clear about procedures for these aspects and also clear about their role in 'monitoring the monitoring'. This is particularly important when targets for pupils with SEN fall outside mainstream indicators. Both Early Learning Goals and National Curriculum level descriptors make it relatively easy to pinpoint achievement and set targets, but if these indicators do not apply they have to be replaced by something which is equally well understood. What is more, the possibility of inconsistent judgements and conflicts of opinion increases in proportion to lack of 'criterion clarity'. SENCOs must rely on colleagues making judgements by proxy, so it is worth spending time ensuring that the criteria for judging progress are clear and unambivalent. It is also worth considering what role learning support or classroom assistants will play.

TASK 33

Establishing monitoring criteria

Identify those targets for pupils with SEN which fall outside national performance indicators.

Write the equivalent of level descriptors which enable judgements to be made about progress towards targets (for example, the criteria for judging acceptable and unacceptable behaviour).

Establish a clear policy for how and when progress will be assessed and recorded.

Decide how you are going to monitor the process.

Table 6.1 summarises all these management functions in the form of a checklist so that newly appointed SENCOs can judge what is already in place and what developments are needed.

TABLE 6.1 Management functions checklist

FUNCTION	IN PLACE ✔	NOT IN PLACE ✘
Ensuring that SEN pupils are included in overall school targets		
Setting targets outside mainstream national indicators		
Pupils and parents consulted when targets are set		
Teachers' additional workload managed		
Early warning system on poor progress established		
Teachers know and understand all targets		
Complementary process targets established		
Targets for SEN part of school self-review		
Professional development needs identified		
Objectives clear within SEN development plan		
SEN targets interpreted in subject development plans		
SEN given due prominence in school development plan		
Structural targets set as well as pupil targets		
Parents clear about role in helping to meet targets		
Systems for consistent monitoring of progress clear		
SENCO's 'monitoring of monitoring' procedures clear		
The school SEN policy gives a commitment to target setting		

Make sure that any items marked X – *'not in place'* – go into the SENCO Personal Action Plan at the end of Chapter 2.

———— Targets for the whole curriculum ————

The purpose of this chapter has been to outline the main management functions which characterise the role of the SENCO in the process of target setting. This final short section concentrates on the four main types of targets commonly set for pupils with special educational needs. The management functions need application and adaptation to each type, but SENCOs should strive to uphold these principles as their main goal:

- targets for pupils with SEN must be seen as integral to the whole school targets for improvement and their value clearly demonstrated;

- targets are not isolated from daily classroom practice as if they have an independent existence, they must be seen as part of the SENCO's insistence upon the non-acceptance of low standards;

- SEN targets must be just as rigorous and demanding as any other school targets.

TASK 34

Managing different types of targets

Refer to Table 6.1 on page 143 and the Personal Action Plan at the end of Chapter 2 on page 29 as you read the next pages.

List the management tasks needed for successful implementation of each of the target categories which follow.

Types of targets

General curriculum targets are those which have a bearing on how a child or pupil performs across the whole curriculum. They may complement other targets which use national benchmarking by concentrating, for example, on specific aims to improve standards of literacy and numeracy, or they may focus on generic skills such as presentation, problem-solving, working collaboratively or improving concentration span. These targets will involve discussion with all subject or class teachers and the system of monitoring and recording progress needs consistent application. Each subject or class will need frequent re-visiting to assess the impact of the targets across a wide range of learning situations and the SENCO will need reliable and accurate information from colleagues. IEPs lend themselves ideally to these targets and their main application should be to pupils on Stages 2 and 3 of the current Code of Practice five stage model. The replacement of this model with a probable two stage version under the revised Code of Practice means that SENCOs will need to apply these targets to the equivalent groups of pupils.

Specific curriculum targets focus on areas of need related to how the skills of a particular subject are acquired and practised. They may equally apply to pupils identified as being at Stage 1 because of learning difficulties in a relatively narrow range of skills or to gifted and talented children who need to extend and develop advanced skills in one or more curriculum areas. Heads of department or curriculum coordinators should be instrumental in setting these targets and schemes of work should be sufficiently differentiated to allow lessons to absorb the needs of individual pupils. Subject-based reports to parents will need modification to include scope for commenting on targets.

Whole child targets can be applied to children or pupils at any key stage or register stage. They can be related to academic targets such as reading fluency, handwriting or spoken language skills, or be concerned with personal development such as attitude, behaviour or forming relationships. These targets often form the basis of a statement and other professional advice and input is usually needed from both inside and outside the school. Homework completion, meeting deadlines, attendance and punctuality to lessons are further examples of appropriate targets in this category. Additionally, where schools have pupils with a physical disability or there is a separate unit for sensory impairment, these targets are a useful addition to the range available.

Non-benchmark targets are primarily designed for pupils in special schools, certain categories of statemented pupils and those achieving below National Curriculum level 2. SENCOs and other teachers need guidance on the application of these targets and how often scarcely perceptible progress is described and measured. If SENCOs have pupils who fall into this category then further study is required of a wide range of publications which deal specifically with this area. (I recommend *Supporting the Target Setting Process – guidance for effective target setting for pupils with special educational needs* published jointly by QCA and DfEE, available from DfEE Publications Centre.)

It is not the intention to present this range of targets as mutually exclusive. On the contrary, the decision faced by most SENCOs is which *combination* of targets is appropriate to each child or pupil. For example, a pupil with emotional and behavioural difficulties may well have targets related to improving attitudes and relationships but may also be quite capable of meeting nationally benchmarked targets in most curriculum areas. SENCOs need to decide which combination will motivate the pupil most effectively. For pupils with SEN the most effective combination has been found to be one which is comfortably achieved and one which provides real challenge.

The result of this is a set of targets unique to each child, unlike other school targets which may apply to whole groups of pupils. Nor will the targets fit neatly into a key stage or be containable within classes or subjects. The challenge for SENCOs is to manage this process within the guidelines of this chapter, and have it reflected in the school SEN policy.

TASK 35

Group targets

Examine carefully the range of targets set for pupils with SEN. Are there any patterns or trends?

Discuss with subject or class teachers how some targets can be grouped or whether a number of pupils have very similar targets pitched at more or less the same level.

Devise a system by which teachers and pupils can work together collectively, including aspects such as withdrawal and how support staff are deployed, to meet group targets.

_____ Summary _____

- Target setting is integral to strategies for school improvement and applies equally to all pupils, including those with special educational needs.

- Targets solely related to pupils' attainment outcomes will achieve nothing unless accompanied by 'process' targets which are aimed at creating the condition for success.

- SENCOs need to establish the value placed by the school on targets which fall outside national benchmarks and the best way to achieve this is through development planning.

- It is important that pupils, parents and teaching colleagues understand the targets which are set and appreciate that individual children may have targets selected from a range of categories.

- Effective target setting for pupils with SEN places demands on the management, negotiation and persuasion skills of SENCOs and it is important to understand these functions and have systems in place.

_____

Managing your inspection

Introduction

This is the largest chapter and it brings together many of the features of earlier chapters by concentrating on how SENCOs should respond to the objective evaluation of their work carried out during an OFSTED inspection. The main theme of the chapter is a demonstration of how SENCOs can best manage the inspection process to show themselves, their colleagues and the school as a whole in its best light, while at the same time allowing inspectors the scope to judge how the effectiveness of special needs provision can improve and develop. As with other chapters, the emphasis is on management tasks, responsibilities and duties.

A summary of the main management learning points, incorporating advice on possible actions needed, is given at the end of the chapter. Application of the principles discussed and illustrated to the context of a real inspection provides an ideal test of management development progress and an impartial assessment of future training needs.

Key inspection judgements and approaches

In the period since the inception of the OFSTED inspection system, the process has been revised and refined extensively. Her Majesty's Inspectors of Schools have been responsible for producing the overall guidance for inspectors on what should be the key questions, the nature of the evidence to be investigated and the models for reporting on findings. This guidance is known as the 'Framework for Inspection' and to date there have been three such Frameworks. The first lasted from 1993 to 1996, the second from 1996 to December 1999, and the third and current Framework began life in January 2000. One of the chief characteristics of the process of revision has been to regard many more aspects of school life as *interrelated issues* rather than separate topics so that fewer and fewer sections of inspection reports are compartmentalised. For example, in very early inspection reports on subjects a strict formula was adhered to whereby one paragraph would make judgements about the progress pupils were making and another paragraph would comment on the quality of teaching as if the one had no bearing on the other. Current guidance to inspectors is to *decompartmentalise* and show precisely how strands interrelate. In other words progress is good *because* teaching is good, pupils behave well *because* lessons are stimulating and pupils know exactly what is expected of them.

Similarly, more issues are now regarded as 'whole school' issues and are the responsibility of the whole team of inspectors rather than one member. The prime examples of this are Literacy, Numeracy, the use of Information and Communications Technology across the curriculum, Assessment and its use for target setting and curriculum planning and, of course, Special Educational Needs. The reverse side of the coin is obvious: if certain issues are inspected by the whole team, they must be the responsibility of the whole school. *Every* teacher in a primary school and *all* subject departments in a secondary school have a responsibility for standards of literacy, for example. This states the glaringly obvious but it has not always been the case in every school. Now, the next assertion is even more important and should be equally obvious: *whole school responsibility entails effective whole school management*. If the school has effective assessment procedures in all subject areas except one or two, it is not the fault of the assessment policy nor the subjects concerned, it is the fault of management for not monitoring the consistent application of the policy with sufficient expertise and rigour. Using 'assessment' as the example again, the progress of refining judgements over the eight or so years of OFSTED inspections can be illustrated by the following questions.

■ What is the school's system for assessment?

■ How good is the assessment process in the school?

■ How is assessment used to inform curriculum planning?

■ How is assessment data used to predict future attainment, set targets for improvement and calculate 'value added'?

■ What is the impact of the school's assessment practice on the standards achieved by children/pupils across the curriculum?

■ How well is assessment managed to ensure consistency of approach and maximum impact on standards in every subject?

Each pair of questions follows the thinking behind each of the three Frameworks.

Although inspections have always been concerned with the pupils' levels or standards of attainment, especially when compared with national 'norms' or expectations, the real thrust of current inspections is to place standards of achievement firmly at the heart of the process and link this irrevocably with teaching. There is, therefore, the fundamental assertion that schools are about teachers teaching and pupils learning – everything else is of lesser importance. Pause awhile to recover from this shock revelation!

TASK 36

Assessing school initiatives

Spend about thirty minutes listing and/or discussing the answers to the following questions about recent developments at your school.

1 Which recent initiatives have directly been about teaching and learning?

2 What has been the impact of these initiatives on the standards of children's/pupils' work?

3 What other recent initiatives have been implemented which have only an oblique connection to teaching and learning?

4 Why was it deemed necessary to introduce these latter initiatives?

5 Which has had the greater impact on school life? Why?

Within each inspection 'Framework' there has been an 'Inspection Schedule'. This lists all the areas which must be inspected and the numerical order in which the school's report contains the inspection findings. Annex 1 at the end of this chapter lists the inspection schedule applicable from January 2000 and illustrates how all issues are seen to be interrelated. It also shows, to extemporise upon the ultimate commandment in George Orwell's *Animal Farm*, that 'all issues are important but some issues are more important than others'. Additionally, the latest inspection framework creates the concept of 'short' inspections lasting only two or three days with much smaller teams of inspectors. These inspections apply to schools already deemed 'successful' or which have made significant improvements. The difference between *full* and *short* inspections is more fully explained in Annex 2, together with the implications for SENCOs of short inspections.

So far, this part of the chapter has focused on the approach of inspectors, summarised thus:

■ looking at the relationship between or interrelatedness of issues;

- looking for where issues have a bearing on the whole school;

- assessing the responsibility of management for system failure or the level of contribution to success; and

- relating everything to the quality of teaching and learning.

It's rather like a jigsaw puzzle: all the pieces are there and interconnect to form a total picture, the school has an image of itself but the inspectors do not have the picture on the box – their task is to create it.

Using the information thus far, the aspirant or novice SENCO will have begun to come to some important conclusions. These should be the main ones:

- it does not take OFSTED to tell schools what are or are not whole school issues, schools can and should do this for themselves;

- when things do not quite go completely right is it always fair to blame management?

- standards of academic attainment are not necessarily the most important issues facing special needs teachers.

And, more positively related to the inspection process, these questions:

- is special needs really seen as a whole school issue in the school, which implies a consistent and uniform application of policy and procedure by all teachers?

- what is the level of knowledge and commitment of senior management which underpins the SENCO role?

- is sufficient attention paid by all teachers or subject departments to the processes by which teachers teach and pupils learn in each curriculum area?

- what are the successes directly attributable to intervention by the SENCO and what deficiencies exist as a result of a lack of a suitable intervention strategy?

Inspectors will either ask these questions or deduce the answers.

All of this leads us to conclude that the first key judgement which inspectors have to make is:

> *To what extent is special educational needs seen as a whole school issue in this school?*

To make this judgement clearer in the mind of the SENCO, the following checklist provides a self-analytical model; see Table 7.1 which follows.

TABLE 7.1 Whole school issue descriptors

	Tick as appropriate		
	YES	NO	SPORADIC
1. There is a whole school policy of which everybody is aware.			
2. Senior management meets SENCO formally to review current position, progress of pupils, resources.			
3. Senior management includes SEN as an agenda item in all relevant meetings, especially ones with a focus on curriculum and pupils' attainment.			
4. Subject areas discuss SEN and include in subject development plans.			
5. Teachers have a copy of the register and know the pupils in each class who are on it and at what stage.			
6. The whole school development plan has a section on SEN or SEN is included in each development area.			
7. Senior management lends weight to liaison with LEA, education psychologist and other external agencies.			
8. Adequate time is allocated for testing, parental interviews, annual reviews and case conferences.			
9. Governors play an active role in SEN matters and fully report SEN in their annual report to parents.			
10. All funding specifically allocated to SEN is spent on SEN.			
11. SEN is fully staffed by suitably qualified teachers and an adequate number of classroom or learning support assistants.			
12. Curriculum and assessment plans fully integrate the requirements of pupils with SEN.			
13. SEN pupils are integrated into every aspect of school life, including target setting and extra curricular activities.			
14. Teachers' lesson planning incorporates the needs of all pupils.			
15. SEN is given appropriate prominence in all handbooks, prospectuses to parents, award ceremonies and other external communications.			
16. SENCO has permanent membership of all subject and welfare-based committees or working groups.			
17. IEPs are frequently referred to and there is a section on subject-based targets.			
18. Each subject area allocates a portion of capitation to SEN.			
19. The school provides specialist accommodation and equipment.			
20. SENCO has clear line management, appraisal and professional development opportunities.			

No doubt others may seek to include other characteristics of a whole school issue, for example, whether an individual governor or governors' sub-committee is given a specific brief for oversight of review and development; whether monitoring and evaluation of the topic are the province of, and included in the job description of, a member of the senior management team; or whether the input of specialist advice is sought on issues relating to wider school concerns such as attendance and behaviour. Suffice to say that the checklist given in Table 7.1 gives a comprehensive enough set of criteria to enable SENCOs to judge for themselves whether their area of responsibility is truly, transparently and manifestly a whole school concern, substantiated by fact. Analysis of answers will reveal the points at which pressure should be exerted and should form the basis of an action plan. More than five 'no' answers and more than ten 'sporadic' answers indicate that the school does not take the issue of special needs sufficiently seriously.

It is important for the management work of SENCOs that the school takes the issue of Equal Opportunities seriously. Apart from the clear obligation to comply with statute by ensuring there is no discrimination on the grounds of gender, race, creed or disability, the main point for SENCOs to be aware of is equality of access to the curriculum. The *intention* must be that all children/pupils have equal access to the whole curriculum and so SENCOs must be familiar with the curricular demands, including the National Curriculum, of each subject. We have to remember the possible range of special needs, including those of the gifted pupils and those with physical or sensory impairment. Inclusion will have a profound impact here. Central to the work of all SENCOs is the coordination of provision across the whole curriculum, and as an essential precursor to managing curricular provision effectively a firm principle must be established in the culture and value system of the school. This may stretch the SENCO's powers of persuasion to the limit and makes it all the more vital that senior management is on board. *The relationship between pupils with special needs and the curriculum is not a pupil-centred problem, it is a curriculum-centred one. SENCOs should not be expending energy on trying to fit pupils into the curriculum because colleagues claim they have no room to manoeuvre, that energy should be spent on adapting the curriculum.*

The question of whole child/whole curriculum proactive management is covered in more detail in the Tailpiece (see page 207), but for the purposes of preparing for OFSTED inspectors' enquiries, the following guidance should be studied and acted upon. If we ask the question – 'Do all children/pupils have equal access to the whole curriculum?' – the likely answer in all schools will be 'No'. If we ask the question – 'Is the SENCO influencing curriculum provision so as to maximise the opportunities for pupils with special needs to participate in the full curriculum?' – the answer most definitely should be 'Yes'.

The first step in problem solving, and a recurring theme throughout this book is *first analyse the problem*. During an inspection week inspectors are attempting to experience the curriculum from the children's point of view and this very often takes the form of 'tracking' a particular pupil or group of pupils with special needs for a day or at the very least across two or three different subject areas. *Arrange to do the same.* You will find a patchy picture across subject areas even in a primary school where only one or two teachers may be involved. In secondary schools note those subject areas where differentiation is by outcome only and where teachers have planned what they are to teach and what the class will do, rather than what learning the lesson is designed to promote. Observe children at break or playtime and during the lunch period: are they isolated or integrated into the activities of other children? Do they seek refuge in a particular area or with an adult? Do they misbehave or are they victims of exclusion, bullying or name-calling? Note any 'personality changes', for example, the boy who is diffident and lacking in confidence in the classroom who is suddenly ebullient and aggressive in a playground game, or the girl who suddenly cries a lot.

> *Record your findings carefully and accurately and arrange to discuss them with senior or line managers.*

Next, complete the curriculum audit in Table 7.2 on page 158. This enables SENCOs to focus on those areas of the curriculum where more work is needed to ensure flexibility of approach. Alternatively, work with a colleague or better still a team of learning support assistants to answer the following questions in a professional development exercise.

TASK 37

Curriculum provision

With colleagues discuss these questions about curriculum provision for pupils with special needs.

Spend about one hour on this.

 What arrangements are made for pupils who suffer an injury or illness such that they need to spend long periods of time at home or in hospital, or who have temporary restricted movement around school?

 Which subjects have a curriculum content which habitually reinforces a sense of failure in pupils?

3 Is it or would it be possible for pupils with a physical or sensory impairment to participate in such subjects as physical education, drama, music or design technology? Do they?

4 Are withdrawal arrangements such that pupils always miss the same lessons or even whole subjects?

5 Are the grounds for disapplication of the National Curriculum based on pupils' needs or some perceived difficulty with a particular subject? Is this decision secure or a breach of opportunity?

6 Which subjects or which teachers plan or do not plan work in conjunction with classroom assistants?

7 What are the opportunities for subject content in the targets in IEPs?

The completion of the discussion exercise or the provision audit table enables SENCOs to test their knowledge of the curriculum, leads to a greater appreciation of the problems faced by subject colleagues and indicates where the pressure points should be. Discussion with colleagues is vital if a full picture of the curriculum is to be established and if SENCOs are to get an accurate 'fix' on the attitudes of teachers towards seeking greater subject adaptability. Discussion with the children themselves will complete the picture and provide valuable insights into *their* perception of what each subject allows them to do and the reasons why they are making greater or lesser progress.

In relation to provision for pupils with Statements of Special Educational Need, note that there is an obligation to ensure that the curriculum followed by pupils is compatible with the provision specified in the statement. Therefore the provision audit should be carried out for these pupils if for no others, though the table headings may need adaptation.

We can now note three more key judgement areas to be investigated by OFSTED inspectors:

To what extent do pupils with special educational needs have access to the whole school curriculum?

What provision is made in each curriculum area for pupils with special needs?

Does curriculum provision match the requirements of statements?

TABLE 7.2 Curriculum provision audit

CURRICULUM SUBJECTS	ACCESSIBILITY JUDGEMENTS				
	Full	Partial	None	Can do work from higher/lower key stage	Good range of methods for differentiation	Specialist resources or equipment available

English

Mathematics

Science →

Complete the list in full

Provision, of course, is more than just what happens in the subjects of the curriculum. Inspectors are concerned with *all* the arrangements which the school has in place to cater for the needs of pupils. For example, if the school houses a specialist unit for which the SENCO may or may not be responsible, some important judgements will have to be made about the efficient management of the unit and its effectiveness in terms of what pupils can achieve. Even if the unit is headed and staffed by specialists, the SENCO is responsible for the coordination of all special needs provision and is, therefore, the point of liaison between the unit and the main school curriculum. Nor is it safe to assume that children have only one obvious problem or need: it is perfectly possible for a child in a specialist visual impairment unit, for example, to have a different learning or behavioural problem or display gifted talents for, say, music. There must be clearly demonstrable links between the work of a unit and that of the SENCO, and this demands knowledge of the answers to these questions:

- what are the arrangements for judging the criteria for attendance at the unit?
- how many pupils is the unit designed to take and what is its primary function?
- what arrangements are made for pupils to experience the National Curriculum?
- what are the arrangements for transporting pupils to and from the unit?
- do pupils based in the unit have an opportunity to participate in the wider aspects of school life such as trips and visits or extra curricular activities?
- what are the funding and staffing arrangements?
- are these all external to the school's own finances?
- are pupils attending the unit on the school roll and therefore eligible for inclusion in the special needs register?
- do staff work exclusively in the unit or is there some other arrangement for the allocation of time?
- are pupils in the unit entered for National Curriculum tests or public examinations? Are they recorded as part of the school's results or separately?
- do staff working in the unit need specialist qualifications?
- does the unit follow the timetabled structure of the school day?
- is it just coincidence that the unit occupies accommodation on the school site and is therefore nothing to do with the school?

In the majority of schools, however, there is no separate unit, although many schools have decided to set up an area where pupils with behavioural problems can be temporarily excluded from normal lessons. In this more usual situation, provision for special needs over and above the daily curriculum amounts to the arrangements for spending any specially allocated grants or funds; use of resources, equipment and specialist accommodation; the system for withdrawal from lessons where this occurs; the deployment of classroom assistants; the allocation of specific resources and learning support to statemented pupils; guidance issued to teachers on strategy and differentiated planning; arrangements for continuing professional development of staff; and any particular arrangements made to support pupils, for example, over the production of GCSE coursework in secondary schools.

This leads to the next key judgement question for inspectors:

> *What is the extent of the level of provision for pupils with special needs in addition to that of the subjects of the curriculum?*

The extent to which SENCOs have the answers to the questions raised above and can supply evidence to substantiate them will indicate the extent of management responsibility. Make sure, for example, that there is a clear rationale and consistent system for the deployment of classroom assistants. How do you manage the situation where a learning support assistant is employed specifically to help a statemented pupil and that pupil is absent from school: is there clear guidance for this? Is there evidence that the SENCO has monitored the effects of expenditure of time, resources and funding on pupils' progress?

Before provision can be decided and resources deployed, pupils' needs must be identified. The exact diagnosis of need or confirmation of existing analysis is the first and most important function of the SENCO. This demands the coordination of other people's activities and the examination of a wide range of information. The management processes involved are discussed more fully in Chapter 2, see 'Following appointment' pages 20–22, so for the purposes of managing an OFSTED inspection only the key questions will be covered here. Inspectors need to be satisfied that a proper system is in place to enable pupils' needs to be identified as accurately and as early as possible. Three management processes are in play here simultaneously:

- working in a systematic and structured way with other people, some of whom will be school colleagues and some will not;

- deciding what data and information is necessary, acquiring it, presenting it in an acceptable format and drawing the right conclusions from it;

- making decisions about provision, corrective strategies, use of resources and staff time and monitoring effectiveness.

Guidance on these three areas is in the chapters referred to earlier, but inspectors will be seeking evidence of how quickly, smoothly and efficiently the information is gathered on each pupil to enable the correct provision to be triggered.

FIG. 7.1 Possible sources of information on individual needs

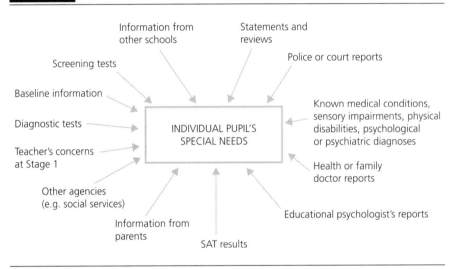

TASK 38

Sources of information

Figure 7.1 illustrates the range and sources of possible information. Use the information in the diagram and your knowledge and experience to complete the checklist given as Table 7.3 on page 162.

TABLE 7.3 Identification of needs information checklist

TYPE OF INFORMATION	SOURCE	WHEN AVAILABLE	USE	WHEN UPDATED	CONFIDENTIAL
Needs analysis	Previous school	July	Pupils grouping CA provision	Termly	✗
Statement	LEA	Current	Curriculum and LSA deployment	Annual review	✗ ✓
Court report	Police liaison	Current	Background, EBD progress report	On-going	✗
Screening tests			Pupil groupings		
Baseline					
Diagnostic tests				Termly	
Stage 1					
Social report	Social services				✓
Personal	Parents				
SAT results		September			✗
Ed. Psych. reports					
Medical					
School tests	October		Set movement intervention	Annual	✗
Case conference	Multi agency				✓
IEP	SENCO		Daily teaching, targets for learning		

The completion of the table enables the SENCO to check that the school is making proper use of all the information available and demonstrates the need to coordinate not only the data but the means of acquiring it. In secondary schools this issue is sometimes particularly acute because of a lack of consistent approach from a potentially large number of 'feeder' junior schools. In a situation where the SENCO feels that transfer information is incomplete or displays a wide variety of quantity and quality, there are two practical remedies:

- meet with SENCO colleagues in junior schools in order to devise common transfer systems (the LEA should already be doing this!);

- devise screening tests for all Year 7 pupils or use test packages already commercially available.

It is important for SENCOs in all phases of education to remember that a key management function centres around the efficient transfer of information to colleagues in the next phase so as to ensure the continuation of specialist provision without the need for continual re-testing and re-diagnosis of need.

These points are encompassed by the next key judgement area for inspectors:

> *What is the accuracy, reliability, and range of incoming and outgoing information to enable children's/pupils' special needs to be identified clearly and quickly?*

Although each of the three inspection 'Frameworks' has varied the approach of inspectors to SEN, the basic requirement to investigate and report on

IDENTIFICATION ⟶ PROVISION ⟶ OUTCOME

has remained constant. As Chapter 4 showed (see 'Policy formulation and implementation', page 71), it is useful to take this three part view of school policy formulation as a model since it also matches OFSTED's expectations. We have now covered the key judgements to be made by inspectors in relation to identification and provision, let us turn finally to outcome.

The judgements in relation to how pupils respond to their needs being identified and provided for are the same for SEN pupils as for all other children at school:

- how do pupils react in terms of attendance, behaviour and attitudes to learning?

- what standards do pupils achieve in relation to National Curriculum levels or examination grades?

■ how do standards compare with what you would expect, given levels of prior attainment (and nature of special need)?

■ are pupils progressing as well as, better, or worse than expected?

■ what are the strengths and weaknesses in what pupils know, understand and can do?

Underpinning each of these questions is *why*? What accounts for these standards? What is it about teaching which results in better/worse than expected progress by pupils with special needs towards the targets set for them? What is it about the management and coordination of SEN which makes standards in this school better/worse than in similar schools with pupils with similar needs?

As stated earlier in this chapter, the standards of pupils' achievements are at the very core of inspections, and everything else is judged for its impact on those standards. So, for example, as an efficient SENCO you will have a good system for filing pupils' records, including secure storage of information relating to statements and reviews. However, it is not the efficient system which counts, it is *the effective use to which it is put* to improve the process of teaching and learning. SENCOs should ask themselves these questions about their record-keeping systems and correct deficiencies:

■ are records accurate and up to date?

■ are they in a format which is easy to follow?

■ are they identified according to the stages of the Code of Practice? (See Chapter 3: 'Theoretical basis', page 37 for an explanation of Code of Practice stages.)

■ do they match the purpose for which they are intended?

■ are they fully accessible to those who need to see and use them?

■ can they be used to record gains in attainment and hence track the rate and nature of progress?

■ are they used to set targets; deploy resources and staff; plan lessons or other provision; inform assessments or reviews; as a basis for discussions or curriculum development; to identify professional development needs in colleagues; or to move pupils on to, out of or within stages?

Record-keeping is used just as an example here, the same could be said for resources for learning – what is the actual impact on the quality of teaching and learning, as shown by the standards achieved, of using this particular set of materials as opposed to not using them?

As SENCO, you need to be absolutely clear about the extent of the impact on standards of everything for which you are responsible. You also need to have well documented evidence of any negative impact on standards of anything for which you are not responsible but which forms part of the whole school approach – accommodation and funding spring to mind immediately here, as does allocation of non-contact time. Figure 7.2 on page 166 shows those aspects which directly impact upon standards of achievement. Study this diagram and complete the professional development exercise which now follows. The diagram includes items which SENCOs may not be responsible for providing, but which they may well be responsible for using to maximum effect or, at the very least, influencing their use.

TASK 39

Strengths and weaknesses

SENCOs should complete this on their own or in discussion with colleagues as part of a staff training day.

Spend about two hours recording findings.

1 On a piece of paper (or flip chart) draw up two columns, headed Strengths and Weaknesses.

2 Assess each of the aspects which appear in the diagram in Fig. 7.2 for their impact on the educational standards achieved by pupils with special needs. Include the full range of special needs, including giftedness, where appropriate. Remember, do not judge the quality of the aspect, judge its *impact*.

3 Note the main strengths and weaknesses of each aspect in relation to impact on standards.

4 Record major weaknesses as items for future discussion and action planning.

Finally, the standards themselves. Given that special needs has a wide definition to include gifted pupils, it is perfectly possible to evaluate standards in terms of known measures. Similarly, all pupils have an entitlement to follow the National Curriculum and that includes statutory assessment at the end of the key stages. Attainment is always judged against expectations, and for many pupils in the secondary phase this includes vocational qualifications as well as other forms of accreditation. For the majority of pupils with special needs the learning difficulties experienced render comparisons with national norms meaningless. The issue is one of progress and the 'value' added by the school. SENCOs need to be clear about each pupil's capacity to achieve and to be able to substantiate this with evidence of prior attainment and rates of progress. It is important to be able to identify accurately the level pupils are currently achieving and what they are working towards. In absolute terms, of course, standards will be below national norms, but does this represent high enough standards? In other words should the pupil at level 2 really be at level 3 or does level 2 show excellent progress from a very low base? Does level 7 at the end of Key Stage 3 for a number of pupils indicate a lack of policy for giftedness because there are no level 8s?

FIG. 7.2 Aspects which have an impact on standards of achievement

Inspectors are not bothered about a school's position in 'league tables' or any statistical 'skew' caused by the attainment levels of pupils with special needs. As the professional practitioner a SENCO should be able to demonstrate that the standards achieved (including those for behaviour) are rooted in accurate assessment and are the very best possible in the light of all the evidence. The vital ingredient is leadership by the SENCO in setting high expectations for individual achievement, however low the outcome in 'national average' terms.

The last key judgement, then, and the one which encapsulates all the other inspection judgements is:

How high are the educational and other standards achieved? Are they high enough? Does this represent better or worse than expected progress? What factors account for this?

These seven key judgements are given again in Table 7.4 and taken together they form the basis of a school's special educational needs self-evaluation programme. Table 7.4 concludes this section of the chapter.

TABLE 7.4   The seven key OFSTED judgements

1 To what extent is SEN seen as a whole school issue?

2 To what extent do pupils with SEN have access to the whole school curriculum?

3 What provision is made in each curriculum area for pupils with SEN?

4 Does curriculum and other provision match the requirements of statements?

5 What is the extent of provision for pupils with SEN in addition to that of the subjects of the curriculum?

6 What is the accuracy, reliability and range of incoming and outgoing information to enable pupils' needs to be identified clearly and quickly?

7 How high are the educational and other standards? Are they high enough? What does this show about progress and 'value added'? What accounts for this?

_____ Preparing pre-inspection documentation _____

The previous section of this chapter has explained in detail the kind of judgements inspectors are expected to make and how the management responsibilities of SENCOs are explored through the seven key questions. We now turn to the evidence upon which the judgements about *identification* and *provision* can begin to be made early in the inspection process.

Inspectors simply do not have the time to see and explore everything during the inspection week. One member of the inspection team is designated, in the light of his/her qualifications and experience, to coordinate the work of the team in inspecting the provision for special needs and assessing the progress and standards of pupils' achievements. At the same time, the coordinating inspector will have responsibility for inspecting one or more subjects. So time is very limited. It is important, therefore, that the inspector responsible for special needs is able to form an impression of how well things are done at the school before the inspection proper begins. The quality of information provided, the way it is presented and what it shows about identification, provision and outcome says much about the efficiency and effectiveness of the SENCO and the extent to which the school views special needs as an important central issue. On the basis of the documentation received inspectors can form early hypotheses which are then tested by the inspection itself.

A good example of this is subject development plans. If the school policy for special educational needs indicates that there is a whole school approach and that each subject or class teacher has a responsibility to ensure proper provision, subject inspectors will expect to see this reflected in subject development planning. If this is not the case it indicates a mis-match between policy and practice. SENCOs should ensure that each subject head of department or curriculum coordinator considers special needs carefully when formulating plans for future development. This can be done through a series of meetings, through ensuring that when senior management are setting down the parameters for planning it is clear that SEN must figure, and by sharing an early draft of the SEN development plan with colleagues. One of the most frequent criticisms of SEN provision is not necessarily about quality, it is about consistency.

All inspectors will receive substantial documentation before an inspection and they study it for what it reveals about a wide range of issues. If there is no mention of SEN in significant documents such as development plans or subject handbooks this information will be fed back to the inspector responsible who is then primed to ask pertinent questions of the SENCO in relation to the responsibility for coordinating provision across the whole curriculum. *By now, the message should be clear: demonstrate management capability by ensuring the statements in documents are matched by the practice elsewhere.*

The next section of this chapter touches upon the paperwork which should be available to inspectors during an inspection. Here, the focus is on pre-inspection documents and how SENCOs can ensure these are of the right type and quality. The most important document, of course, is the whole school policy. Having a policy for special needs is a statutory requirement and this is covered extensively in Chapter 4, see 'Policy formulation and implementation', page 51. However, it is essential that this is presented to inspectors as an up-to-date true reflection of what happens in practice. It is a good idea to review and re-work the policy periodically because practices and circumstances change. Similarly, it is a statutory requirement for the school policy on SEN to appear in the governing body's Annual Report to Parents. *This does not always happen.* There is no need for the whole policy to appear if it is a weighty document, a summary of its main features will do, but there must be an evaluation of the effectiveness of the policy together with a statement about SEN funding arrangements. SENCOs should ensure that these statutory requirements are met and that copies of these reports, say for the past two years, are available to inspectors.

The burden on schools to produce extensive documentation for inspectors has been reduced dramatically as each 'Framework' has come on stream. 'Essentials only' is the rule because inspectors need to use their limited time productively in observing what actually happens. SENCOs need to decide for themselves what it would be useful for inspectors to know beforehand so that time is not wasted in seeking out routine information. Much of the outcome information can be made available and discussed during the inspection. Pre-inspection paperwork should be limited to the identification and provision aspects. It may be, for example, that there is already a SEN handbook which covers all of this. Such a handbook, issued to all teachers and other relevant parties, which expands the detail of the policy by giving both information and guidance, is good practice and enables the SENCO to demonstrate how he/she influences procedure on a school-wide basis. Essential information includes the methods used to identify pupils' individual needs: how and from what sources information is gathered, at what point in the school calendar and how it is subsequently used. Think of ways of presenting this in tabulated form so that it is clear, makes for easy reference and can be reviewed and updated without the need for substantial re-writing. Refer back to Table 7.3 on page 162 for a model for this. Remember, for the purpose of this exercise it is the methods, not the results, which are being demonstrated. A good example, which illustrates both the professional and management role of the SENCO, would be details of any tests, screening or diagnostic which are administered and/or marked by the SENCO. There should be a clear explanation of the purpose of the tests, how the results are interpreted, disseminated and subsequently used (for pupil grouping, curriculum planning, modifications to teaching strategies, target setting and IEPs, deployment of extra support or resources, differentiation and so on), and whether there is any follow-up or re-testing later in the year or term to ascertain progress and hence monitor and evaluate provision. By using documentary examples such as these you are demonstrating to inspectors that you have both the professional knowledge and management expertise to influence the way in which things happen on a broad front. In selecting documentary evidence, the prime concern then is to present management information: what is done, how it is done, why, when, by whom and to what planned effect.

The same criterion applies to documentary evidence about provision. The quality of provision in relation to pupils' exact needs and the progress pupils make towards expected levels of achievement is the prime focus of the inspection itself, so documents which may be useful before an inspection may be limited in scope. Limit pre-inspection documents to those which show the arrangements the school makes to enable pupils with special needs to experience the curriculum at an appropriate level, and the part played by the SENCO in determining and administering those arrangements. For example, a curriculum which is based entirely on mixed ability pupil groups throughout the school, as in many (but not all) primary schools, needs carefully constructed scaffolding to support it. How is that support put together, and by whom? Where pupils are grouped by prior attainment or substantiated perceptions of 'ability', how is teaching in lower (or even upper) sets supported by resources, guidance on strategies, IEPs and classroom assistance? Can the SENCO provide written evidence of the methods and procedures (not results) used to monitor and evaluate the quality and range of provision in all subject areas?

Also under the heading of provision can come other documentary evidence of specific management activities. Examples would include minutes of meetings; staffing structures to include the number, qualifications, deployment and time spent in school of any classroom or learning support assistants and other specialist staff; development or action plans which are linked to specific objectives such as adaptations of the National Literacy or Numeracy Strategies; particular policy initiatives which are planned or are up and running, such as extending the use of information and communication technology; inventories of equipment and resources which show a topic, subject, key stage or particular need (for example dyslexia) focus; and the outcomes of any involvement by governors. This is a good range of evidence which would be useful for an inspector to see as early in the inspection as possible, if not beforehand.

It must be stressed at this point that none of the documents referred to up to this stage should be specifically written for an inspection. They are all valuable management tools, represent and aid efficiency, keep things orderly and systematic (which is vital given the levels of bureaucracy faced by SENCOs) and represent many of the good practices referred to elsewhere in this book. If anything mentioned so far is missing, needs updating or revising, add it to your personal action plan (PAP) shown in the conclusion to Chapter 2, see 'Following appointment', page 29.

Some documents are, however, compiled especially for an inspection and these *must* be available to inspectors in the weeks immediately prior to the inspection itself. These are largely the responsibility of the headteacher, and consist of a series of forms, each of which give a different picture of the school. The forms, prefixed 'S' (for school), are numbered thus:

FORM S1   Gives basic information about the school: name, age range, address and so forth, plus numbers of pupils in each year group, breakdown of ethnic origin, number of teachers and details about the curriculum. *There is also a section for factual details about Special Educational Needs.*

FORM S2   Asks for more specific details about pupils: exclusions by ethnicity; mobility of school population; attendance; percentage of secondary pupils moving on to further or higher education; test and examination results plus targets for improvement; standards of attainment on entry and how subjects are allocated curriculum time. There are further sections on organisation, staffing and finance. *There is a specific section on income and expenditure in relation to Special Needs.*

FORM S3   Is a self-audit and gives the school an opportunity to describe the extent to which it believes it is fulfilling society's expectations. Questions follow the format of the schedule given in Annex 1 to this chapter, see Annex 1, 'New Inspection Framework' schedule from January 2000, page 196. *There are sections of this form which relate to the school's own evaluation of Special Needs provision.*

FORM S4   Enables the headteacher to give her/his view of the school, its successes and areas in need of further development. *There are many sections of this form which provide scope to evaluate the school's approach to Special Needs.*

SENCOs should expect to be consulted over the compilation of these forms, especially when it comes to providing accurate and verifiable figures. Also, it is important that evaluations are realistic and based on hard evidence so that there is no conflict between an inspector's judgements and the school's opinion of itself. The detail of the information provided, and its accuracy, says much about the quality of the SENCO's record-keeping systems. *It is always a key function of good management to be able to supply accurate information to those who may need it to form the basis of strategic decision making.*

This section has described the important documents which, ideally, should be available to inspectors before an inspection begins, and has given some insights into the key management functions which these documents, and the process of their compilation, involve. Table 7.5 which follows summarises the pre-inspection documentation. Please refer to Annex 2 on page 196 for details of the implications for SENCOs of self-evaluation in 'short' inspections.

TABLE 7.5 Pre-inspection documentation checklist

PRE-INSPECTION DOCUMENTS	RESPONSIBILITY	SENCO INPUT	ESSENTIAL	USEFUL
School SEN policy	Governors, SMT, SENCO	✓	✓	
Subject development plans	Heads of subjects/ coordinators	✓		✓
SEN development plan	SENCO	✓	✓	
Subject handbooks	Subject staff	✓		✓
SEN handbook	SENCO	✓	✓	
Governors' Annual Report to Parents	Governors	✓	✓	
Details of identification procedures	SENCO	✓		✓
Tests and assessment methods	SENCO	✓	✓	
Resources, staffing, organisation, timetable and other management information	SMT, SENCO	✓	✓	
Curriculum arrangements including learning support details	SMT, SENCO	✓	✓	
Monitoring and evaluation procedures	SENCO, SMT, SEN governor	✓	✓	
Minutes of meetings	Chairs of groups	✓		✓
Action plans	SENCO	✓		✓
Policy initiatives	SENCO, SMT	✓		✓
■ Staff training and professional development details	SENCO, SMT	✓		✓
■ Cross key stage liaison procedures	SMT, SENCO, Pastoral staff	✓		✓
■ External agency details	SENCO	✓	✓	
■ SEN management structure S1, S2, S3, S4[+]	SMT, SENCO, Headteacher	✓ ✓	✓	✓

[+] See 'Demonstrating good management practice' on page 173.

Demonstrating good management practice

The most effective way to demonstrate good management practice during an inspection is to simply go about your daily work in a normal fashion. Inspectors do not want to see a special show, and they are experienced enough to be able to spot things which have been specially arranged. Besides, the children are apt to let everyone know when something is not normal! Of course, inspections create artificial situations and people must be forgiven for wanting to impress and show off their school in its best light, but the best way to do this is to have good management systems firmly in place and simply let inspectors observe them in operation. Much depends upon the *timing* of an inspection. SENCOs are very busy all the year round, but certain tasks take priority at different times and an inspection should not interfere with the cycle of activities. A SENCO once said to me: "We were due to hold a case conference about a statemented pupil this morning but I've cancelled it because you are here." I asked her why on earth she had done that, it had taken weeks to arrange a suitable time, it was an important meeting and was *precisely* the sort of activity I should like to have seen! So, carry on as normal.

'Management' is an abstract concept, and it exists only through its effects. Inspectors do not have preconceived ideas about particular management systems or leadership styles, they are concerned solely with what works and what doesn't work in the context of the school's unique circumstances. Furthermore, the judgement on leadership and management is not based on notions of good, bad or indifferent, it is based on discernible impact on the quality of teaching and learning. So, for example, what is the good of a superbly well organised filing and record-keeping system if it is never used by teachers to inform their planning so that pupils benefit by making better progress? Good management is best seen in the way it manifests itself in how pupils and teachers go about their daily business. In particular, it is the role played by management systems and the people who operate them in raising standards and accelerating the rates of progress made by pupils which counts most. If the advice given in this book up to now has been absorbed and put into practice, SENCOs will have no difficulty in persuading inspectors of their management skills.

During inspections, ten features in particular should be highlighted:

1 An efficient system for storing and updating pupil records which is *seen* to be used. Teachers and learning support staff should visit the records frequently so as to demonstrate the clear link between a pupil's identified need and the planning of specific provision.

2 Pupils and teachers knowing what they are doing and why. If there is a programme of withdrawal of different groups or individuals at different times for specific corrective work, does this happen smoothly and with minimum disruption of lessons? Do subject or class teachers know about this and plan for it in advance or does it come as a surprise? Are groups of children wandering around apparently aimlessly?

3 Subject or class teachers knowing which pupils in their lessons are on the register, at which stage and for what reasons. Are the right materials or specialised pieces of equipment being used in all lessons, for example, to enable pupils with sensory impairment to fully participate? Are teachers aware of and do they practise a variety of modes of differentiation?

4 Teachers using *consistent* strategies across the whole curriculum for teaching particular individuals or managing their behaviour. Do all teachers adopt the positive 'can do' approach or do some simply tolerate the constant reinforcement of failure and lack of progress? If an inspector decides to 'track' a particular pupil across different areas of the curriculum, what common approaches or inconsistencies will be observed?

5 Individual Education Plans being in evidence consistently across the subjects and teachers. This is not to say that plans for every pupil, in some cases the majority in a class, should be out on the teacher's desk and referred to at every twist and turn of a lesson, that is unrealistic and unreasonable. But teachers should be aware of the contents of IEPs and be able to give details if asked. Is there scope for subject-specific targets? Is there a 'quiet word' with a particular pupil at the end of the lesson to comment (and hopefully praise and encourage) on progress? When work is set during a lesson, are some pupils discreetly reminded about their targets and shown how to meet them?

6 Classroom and learning support assistants being fully integrated into the whole lesson, including planning. Are assistants efficiently deployed in areas where need is greatest? Is proper priority given to statemented pupils and is the support exactly what is required by the terms of the statement? Is there discussion between LSAs and teachers, particularly at the end of lessons, and do LSAs complete a log of what support was given and what progress was made?

7 Pupils with special needs being fully involved. Do they take part in assemblies, read aloud, use the computer, give out the pencils, play the instruments, get parts in the play, go on the trips, have their best efforts put up in displays, play in the school team and get to meet the Lord Mayor?

8 'Bottom sets' in secondary schools getting a good deal. Is the SENCO aware of who teaches lower sets in each subject? Is there a clear rationale, consistently applied, or is it always the least experienced teacher or Buggins' turn? What is the quality of guidance and support? Is help given with the planning of lessons and use of resources?

9 Giftedness being recognised and properly catered for. Is extension work always available? Are talented children given extra opportunities and outlets? Does the system allow or prevent the Year 9 pupil access to A-level mathematics? Is specialised support available for the talented young writer, artist or musician in the same way as it would be for a statemented pupil?

10 'Extras' happening when they should and happening frequently. Is there a properly organised and well-attended homework club? Are older children and adult helpers involved in paired reading? Does the school library cater for lower or higher than average standards of literacy? Do parents visit the school confidently and when it is most convenient for them? Is proper consideration given to work experience placements for older pupils in secondary schools? Does the merit system reward effort and progress?

These ten 'management manifestations' have a number of features in common. First, they are all observable by all inspectors as examples of daily practice in classrooms and around the school generally. Second, they all have an impact on the standards pupils attain and the progress they make – not only standards of academic achievement but standards of self-confidence and self-esteem as well, and they promote positive attitudes to learning. Third, they are all about what *other people* are expected to do, indicating a consistent and coordinated method. Lastly, they all demonstrate that 'management' has already taken place and that practices and procedures are firmly embedded in the school system.

Table 7.6 which follows is a checklist based on these management indicators. Complete the table, discussing items with colleagues where necessary, and note what actions you need to take to ensure these manifestations of SENCO management are part of the routine daily practices in school.

TABLE 7.6 Management indicators audit

MANAGEMENT INDICATOR	INSPECTORS WILL SEE THIS	INSPECTORS WILL NOT SEE THIS	INSPECTORS WILL SEE SOME OF THIS	EXAMPLES OF PARTICULARLY GOOD PRACTICE	ACTION WHICH SENCO OR OTHERS SHOULD TAKE
	✓	✗	✓		
Use of efficient record system					
Everyone knowing what they are doing					
Knowledge of the register					
Consistent strategies					
IEPs being used					
Integration of CAs and LSAs					
Pupils' full involvement					
Good deal for low ability sets					
Giftedness provision					
'Extras' happening					

There are many other ways in which the quality of SENCO management is manifest on a day-to-day basis and which is observable by inspectors. For example, a new policy may have been introduced by the SENCO which has a significant impact on how some teachers approach their work and which may involve extra planning. Let us suppose it has been agreed that all pupils on stages 3 to 5 should produce at least one piece of extended written work each week using a computer. This may be the sort of fresh policy initiative you would wish to highlight during an inspection. In *management* terms the key questions which would need answering would be:

- how was the need for this policy established?
- what is the anticipated outcome in terms of improvements to pupils' standards?
- how many pupils and in which subject areas?
- is the equipment and teaching expertise available?
- after what time interval will the policy be evaluated?
- who will monitor the implementation and by what method?
- at what point and to what extent was senior management involved?
- did the school SEN policy need revising or updating?
- what discussions or consultations took place beforehand? With whom?
- is there complete agreement about the initiative and its timing?
- is there a written record of the decision-making process?

In other words, these are questions about method, impact and 'worthwhileness', three aspects always worth bearing in mind when introducing any new idea.

TASK 40

Management tasks

Spend about three quarters of an hour on this exercise, working on your own.

Identify the management tasks involved in these SENCO responsibilities. (See Chapter 2: Fig. 2.1, page 21 for a list of management tasks.)

 Professional development of colleagues, including LSAs.

 Cross key stage liaison, including between schools.

 Working with external agencies, including the LEA.

 Following the statementing and review procedures.

Which aspects of management identified would be clear to inspectors? Which would need improvement?

The final aspect of management which inspectors need to know concerns the position of the SENCO in the overall management structure of the school. This is often very revealing! Try answering these three questions which I often use in management training sessions in schools.

- Why am I the most important person in the school?
- What would collapse if I wasn't there?
- How easy is it for me to gain instant access to the head?

If you are the head or deputy head of a small primary school and the SENCO role is one which is 'tacked on', in name only, to your other responsibilities simply to comply with statutory regulations, ignore the following because the position in the hierarchy is obvious. If you are not, read on!

The position of SENCO in the management structure of the school sends out a powerful message about the importance the school attaches to special needs. Each school is unique, and every school has its formal and informal power structures whereby someone high up in the formal structure wields very little actual power whereas someone relatively low down in the formal structure could bring the whole place to a standstill if so minded! Where would you place yourself on this scale, taking account of your responsibility, salary and influence on whole school matters? Near the top or near the bottom?

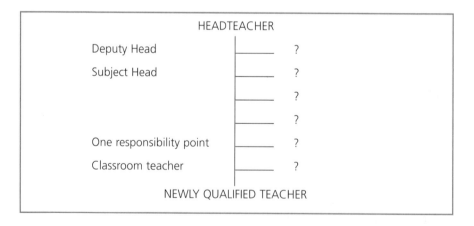

There are, thankfully, rare cases where the SENCO is not on the scale at all! As one headteacher of a grammar school said to me during an inspection: 'We don't have a SENCO because we don't have any special needs.' Oh, really?

This section of the chapter has shown that 'management' is a matter of allowing daily routines and practices to speak for themselves. In a really good football match nobody notices the referee!

———— The issue of standards and progress ————

The standards pupils attain and the progress they make are clearly major issues, and ones which occupy the thinking of SENCOs across the nation. Because this book concentrates on management issues rather than pupil-centred problems, standards of attainment are only fleetingly featured. Moreover, in this chapter on how special needs is inspected it is sufficient to state the OFSTED perception of standards and progress and how inspectors may go about forming a judgement on each. It should be obvious to SENCOs by now though that judgements which inspectors make are about the interrelatedness of issues, and that standards and progress cannot be viewed independently of what brings them about.

It will be helpful at this point to note what OFSTED says about standards in relation to pupils with special needs. In the new Framework, pupils' attainments are viewed in two ways, categorised as *standards* and *achievements*. Standards are defined as *the educational attainment of pupils in relation to some clear benchmark, such as National Curriculum levels, or descriptions, at the end of a key stage*. Achievement reflects *the accomplishments of pupils in relation to what you would expect of those particular pupils*. Inspectors must answer the questions: 'How high are the standards?' and 'How well do pupils achieve?' and both these questions apply to pupils with special needs. This is particularly important to realise in the context of the full range of needs, including pupils with physical, sensory or emotional and behavioural difficulties who may well be working at national standards. It is also important to note that these two aspects of attainment are not separate judgements but are linked by the question of progress. So, pupils with moderate or specific learning difficulties may well be producing work of a standard below national averages but be *achieving appropriately* and making good progress towards the targets in their IEPs. In this context targets could be physical or personal as well as learning ones.

In the situation where standards are particularly low or exceptionally high, the issue for inspectors becomes one of progress. '*Is progress good enough?*' At this point the quality of the SENCO's management of curriculum provision and all the procedures governing the use of IEPs, statement reviews, target setting and recording and monitoring pupils' progress comes under close scrutiny. This is because inspectors need to account for *why* progress is or is not sufficiently good. In other words, it is not what pupils know, understand and can do, it is these things in relation to what is provided for them and the demands which are placed upon them.

Although inspectors' judgements on standards will be summative, based on samples of pupils in larger schools, specific mention will be made of individual curriculum areas where a pattern of inconsistency emerges. So, for example, if pupils are judged to be making good progress in basic literacy but poor progress in history, what is it about the teaching of history which fails to reinforce pupils' clear gains elsewhere? *What aspect of the SENCO's responsibility is not being carried out consistently across the whole curriculum?*

The whole question of progress was discussed at length in the previous chapter, see Chapter 6: 'Setting targets to raise the standards of pupils' achievements', page 131, so in relation to OFSTED inspectors' judgements on the standards and achievements of pupils with special needs, the following *management* tasks and responsibilities are particularly important. Please refer to Table 7.7 which follows and gives the areas to consider and examples of the actions SENCOs may need to take.

TABLE 7.7 Management tasks in relation to standards

MANAGEMENT TASK	POSSIBLE ACTION NEEDED
Recording progress	Pupils' records systematically updated by teachers and assistants to indicate gains in knowledge and skills. Clear link to IEP targets where appropriate. Establish procedure for this and do spot checks.
Consistent use of IEPs	Ensure all teachers are aware of targets and structure work and assessments accordingly. Make a check on homework set/done against targets. Summary of targets to be included in teachers' mark books or lesson planners.
Reinforcement of basic skills	Issue weekly bulletin on skills to reinforce. Link to literacy or numeracy, for example 'This week Year 6 are learning about commas, please emphasise this in lessons and written work set.'
Differentiated planning	Give sample lesson plan based on expected outcomes in learning for *all*, *most*, *some* of class. Observe how lessons are planned in different subjects, especially those outside areas of personal expertise.

Maintaining high expectations	Discuss self-fulfilling prophecies with colleagues; do we expect (and therefore get) too little from some pupils? Focus on pupils who seem to achieve differently in different subjects as examples.
Resource availability	Advertise the resources you have available for others to use. Hold workshop sessions with colleagues to produce subject worksheets with 'simple language/demanding task' style.
Guidance on teaching strategies	Issue guidelines on tackling common problems such as spelling, reading, number work, dyslexia. Hold 'case conference' of all teachers who teach a particular pupil or group to brainstorm good ideas.
Development planning	Ensure all objectives in development plans are linked to teaching, learning and raising standards. Have one central issue which will profoundly influence progress.

Many SENCOs are rightly proud of the relationships and caring ethos which they have helped to shape in their schools, but these must be seen as factors which contribute to the higher priority of *how* pupils learn, *what* they learn and at what *rate*.

———— Highlighting successes ————

So far, this chapter has shown the sort of demands made by inspectors on the time and professional expertise of SENCOs. This short section shows how a proactive approach cannot fail to impress. An inspection offers the school the opportunity to highlight its successes, and a 'short inspection' is designed specifically to focus on those areas which a school believes it does well. (See Annex 2, page 196.)

Inspections are pre-programmed to produce a report which pinpoints the strengths and weaknesses of everything a school does, so SENCOs should automatically begin to think about *strengths* as soon as the school is earmarked for an inspection – and time is increasingly short under the new Framework!

Reflecting on successes

Spend a few minutes jotting down, in no significant order, aspects of special needs in your school which you think are:

- significant successes – this may be particular pupils or groups;

- areas where progress has been made in relation to plans established previously, for example, advances made towards accomplishing objectives identified in last year's development plan.

The 'successes' you will most likely want to highlight will fall into two categories:

- significant achievements by pupils, particularly as a result of some new method of working or the realisation of an objective;

- a particular milestone reached in a development programme which you have instituted or in which you have been heavily involved;

and examples of these should spring readily to mind. In both cases it should be possible to demonstrate the route taken by SENCO management which has brought about the success. For example, it is particularly important in OFSTED inspections to show clearly *why* pupils are making good progress and what systems are in place or being developed to make progress even better. Try to focus on one or two issues to illustrate improvements of some significance.

As a newly appointed or aspirant SENCO you will not have been in post at the time of the previous inspection, though you may have been at the school. If you have not done so already for other reasons, it is a good idea to study the previous inspection report in detail for references to special educational needs, and to note especially if your area of responsibility was identified as a Key Issue or was highlighted for any reason. Inspectors must report on the extent to which a school has improved since the previous inspection, with particular emphasis on the weaknesses identified at that time. So, if the lack of regard for IEPs was criticised before, and this is *still* the case some years on, any other successes you wish to highlight will not cut much ice!

Remember, it is not just the success or improvement itself which matters, *it is how it came about* which will best illustrate the part you have played and, hopefully, emphasise your management skills. In presenting this to inspectors, whether verbally or in the form of a written document, it is a good idea to follow this model:

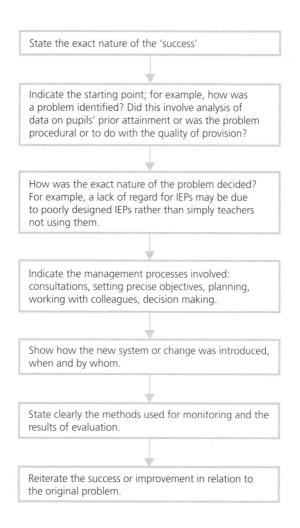

State the exact nature of the 'success'

Indicate the starting point; for example, how was a problem identified? Did this involve analysis of data on pupils' prior attainment or was the problem procedural or to do with the quality of provision?

How was the exact nature of the problem decided? For example, a lack of regard for IEPs may be due to poorly designed IEPs rather than simply teachers not using them.

Indicate the management processes involved: consultations, setting precise objectives, planning, working with colleagues, decision making.

Show how the new system or change was introduced, when and by whom.

State clearly the methods used for monitoring and the results of evaluation.

Reiterate the success or improvement in relation to the original problem.

If this presentation model is supplemented by action plans, sections in development plans, governors' reports or any other documentation, so much the better. Better still if all of it is a clear response to a weakness identified by a previous inspection report!

———— Compliance with statutory requirements ————

As with all aspects of management in schools, the responsibilities and duties of a SENCO are governed by what is useful, what is desirable, what is essential and what is compulsory under statute. The issue of legal requirements and compliance with regulations is covered in more detail in Chapter 3, see 'Synopsis of essential legislation', page 42, but for the purposes of this chapter it is sufficient to note the areas which inspectors will be checking for statutory compliance.

The starting point must be the Code of Practice on the Identification and Assessment of Special Educational Needs itself. (See also Chapter 3 for a full explanation of the Code of Practice.) Although the original 1994 Code is currently being simplified and revised, the principles of the new Code will remain the same as the 1994 one, and the most important principle is that the Code is a statement of good practice, *not* a legally enforceable set of instructions which must be obeyed. The Code takes its strength from the fact that it outlines a clear and sensible system which has resulted in a coherent approach to special needs across the nation and which has enabled pupils to move between schools or between areas of the country and still be protected by the same procedures. Further strength is derived from the fact that the Code of Practice has its origins in statute. The Education Act of 1993 charged the Secretary of State with the task of issuing a Code of Practice so there is a clear statutory *spirit* about it. Moreover, while not statutory in itself, the COP does *contain* some features which *are* statutory, so there is another source of strength.

Schools must 'have regard to' the Code of Practice, and inspectors will need to be satisfied that this is the case. There is nothing to prevent local education authorities and even individual schools from adapting the Code to suit local circumstances and there are many examples of where, for instance, the 'five stage model' has been expanded or contracted to produce a model with fewer or more stages, or where an alternative has been found to the rather unsatisfactory 'awaiting assessment' description given to stage 4. Inspectors will judge that a school does 'have regard to' the Code of Practice if:

- *an individual or group of teachers is identified as having the role of coordinating curriculum provision;*

- *there is an effective system for identifying pupils with special educational needs;*

- *details of these pupils are kept on a register;*

- *careful records are kept and regularly updated;*

- *pupils are categorised according to the extent of their need and the specialised support provided;*

- *resources and teaching methods are suitably modified to take account of the needs of all pupils;*

- *the progress of pupils with special needs is regularly assessed, resulting in clear targets for improvement.*

The two most significant aspects of the Code of Practice which carry statutory force are that the school must have a policy on special educational needs and that the governing body must report on that policy. The governors' role is covered as part of their wider statutory role anyway, but specifically under the Education (Special Educational Needs) (Information) Regulations 1994 governing bodies are obliged to make the policy available. Details of what that policy should contain are given in Chapter 4, see 'Policy formulation and implementation', page 61. The 1994 Regulations also make it clear that the governors' Annual Report to Parents *must* include information on:

■ the success of the SEN policy;

■ significant changes in the policy;

■ any consultation with the LEA, the funding authority and other schools;

■ how resources have been allocated to and amongst children with special educational needs over the year.

This full reporting by the governing body is the most frequent statutory breach observed by inspectors in all schools.

There are all sorts of statutory regulations concerning the way schools are funded and how schools allocate and spend their money. The basic check made by inspectors in respect of special educational needs is one of compliance with Part III of the Education Act 1993. Under this element of statute schools are required to use the funds devolved to them for special educational needs to ensure that:

■ provision matches need;

■ resources are used efficiently;

■ other children are educated efficiently.

With regard to the extent to which there is an effective policy for equal opportunities in the school, SENCOs should be aware of the principle established by section 36 of the Education Act 1944 and later reinforced by the Children Act 1989. In essence this principle is that all pupils are entitled to efficient full-time education suitable to their age, abilities, aptitudes and any special educational needs they may have. The entitlement goes beyond the mere absence of discrimination and includes how certain groups of pupils are to be supported in gaining access to the curriculum.

The Code of Practice makes it quite clear that its purpose is to advise and give examples of best practice, not to prescribe. Until, that is, we come to the question of what happens at stages 4 and 5. The proper name for Stage 4 is *Statutory Assessment* and what happens at this and the statement stage is governed by very strict regulations. Inspectors need to be sure that the procedures for formally assessing a pupil's needs, and then issuing a statement which determines how those needs are to be best met, are properly and thoroughly administered. Although much of the responsibility lies with the local authority once the formal referral for assessment has been made, nevertheless the onus is on the school, and hence the SENCO, for ensuring that all the procedures have been followed and provision is strictly in accordance with the terms of the statement. Inspectors will examine a sample of statements, the number of which depends on how many pupils have statements. If there are five or fewer pupils with statements, the inspector will examine all statements and reviews. If there are more than five pupils with statements, at least half will be scrutinised. When there are large numbers with statements, a sample of not less than five per cent will be seen. They will also quiz SENCOs about procedures for reviews. All these procedures come under section 168 of the Education Act 1993 and the Education (Special Educational Needs) Regulations 1994. Critical for SENCOs, for example, will be the arrangements for consulting with parents.

Neither inspectors nor SENCOs can be expected to memorise the fine detail of all statutory regulations, but schools cannot afford to be in breach of any of them.

The final area covered by statutory regulations which affects the work of SENCOs is the question of disapplications from the National Curriculum. Only headteachers have the authority to modify pupils' entitlements to the full National Curriculum, but more often than not this is done after consultation with, or on the recommendation of, the SENCO. There are two reasons for this: first because the pupils being disapplied are at stages 3, 4 or 5 of the Code of Practice and second because there must be *specific* alternative curriculum provision, not just sitting in the library while the rest do French! The Education Act 1996 sets down the regulations for this. The National Curriculum may be disapplied for pupils with statements under section 354, and section 365 allows the headteacher to make a temporary disapplication for pupils who may, for example, be at Stage 4 awaiting a statement, or who are at risk of exclusion.

Use Table 7.8 which follows as a quick reference point when checking that everything is in place to deal with inspectors' awkward questions.

TABLE 7.8 Statutory requirements spot check

	Y/N
'Having regard to' the Code of Practice	
Detailed whole school policy on special needs	
Full reporting of policy by governing body	
Proper use of specific devolved SEN funding	
Equal opportunities legislation met in full	
Statutory assessment and statementing correct	
Disapplication procedures followed	

——— Evaluating policy and practice ———

Many 'management' tasks in schools amount to little more than overseeing the efficient application of routine administrative procedures. Setting up those procedures in the first place may well have necessitated considerable planning, consultation and the acquisition of resources – all activities which fall within the definition of management – but once the system is in place it simply needs checking for consistency and fine-tuning for improvements to method. A good example would be record-keeping or maintaining the register – administrative tasks which are characterised by their regularity and simplicity. Administrative systems which take up too much of a SENCO's time and which generate mountains of paper are poor systems and leave little time for the two most important functions of a SENCO's role: teaching and evaluating policy.

Think of all the routine administrative tasks connected with SEN in your school which you, as the SENCO, and other colleagues are expected to complete. Answer these questions.

■ *What is the task designed to achieve? What is its purpose?*

■ *Does it achieve that purpose efficiently? Is there a better way?*

■ *Does the task originate in custom and tradition or is there a clear rationale for this practice?*

■ *Is there a clear beneficial link between the task and pupils' learning?*

■ *Is the task 'user friendly' and quick to complete? Or is it time-consuming and a real nuisance to chase up?*

- *Is it something which is done well by some people but not by others?*

- *Lastly, is the time spent on the task disproportionate to its importance?*

Whether as a new SENCO you are setting up the role in the school for the first time, or taking over from someone else, it is always a good idea to evaluate the many administrative tasks in the way illustrated by these questions. Try listing all the tasks and applying the questions in the form of a checklist, that way you are evaluating what needs to be done for efficiency.

OFSTED inspectors will be looking closely at the school's overall policy for SEN and matching it to actual practice observed. There is always *some* gap between policy and practice because of the 'human factor', the extent of the gap is the measurement of the quality of management. This is true of all school policies, whatever the topic. There will always be teachers who simply don't do what they are supposed to do in any given circumstance, or who genuinely and fundamentally disagree over procedures. One good example to bear in mind in this respect is how a pupil with a statement for emotional and behavioural difficulties copes with the whole curriculum and a range of teachers. *Consistency* is the key to any behaviour management strategy and the fact that this pupil 'gets away with it' or 'is a real pain' in some lessons but not in others is a sign that the strategy is being applied inconsistently and the pupil is exploiting that fact. A situation like this would also pose a challenge to the effectiveness of the SENCO's monitoring of how the policy is put into practice.

Monitoring and evaluation are two key aspects of management which are closely scrutinised by inspectors because they are the two most obvious management functions of postholders in schools who are otherwise preoccupied with matters of administration. The lack of effective monitoring and evaluation procedures is the most common weakness highlighted by inspectors and many managers in schools, including headteachers, find this hard to take when they are working so hard to run what, on the face of it, seems like an efficient school. Nevertheless, as a SENCO some form of monitoring and evaluation is part of your role and the reason for this is quite obvious: SENCOs are responsible for coordinating provision for SEN and advising colleagues *across the whole curriculum*. While you may be quite comfortable with what happens within your own area, how secure are you with the full and consistent application of the school's policy in *all* subject areas? *Monitoring* asks the questions: 'What are we doing?' and 'Are we doing what we agreed we would do?' *Evaluation* asks the questions: 'Is there a way of measuring our effectiveness?' and 'How do we know whether we are being successful?' Evaluation is important because it can prevent a lot of wasted effort just plodding along doing something simply because 'this is the way it's always been done'; it is an essential precursor to change; and it is *always* the starting point for development planning and target setting. There is no 'right' way to evaluate a policy, it is a question of making informed judgements based on the degree of success in achieving expected outcomes. *Which means the policy, or the practical procedures which underpin it, must be clear from the outset about its predicted effects*, see Chapter 4: 'Policy formulation and implementation', page 66. Governors have a statutory obligation to report to parents on the effectiveness of the school's SEN policy, see 'Compliance with statutory requirements', page 183, which means some evaluation by the SENCO. This is rarely done effectively and even more rarely reported on by governors.

So what should the SENCO actually do? The first step is to open negotiations with the school's senior management because the SEN policy is a whole school document which has had to be ratified by the governing body. There are implications, therefore, if evaluation reveals that the policy needs modification or, in extreme cases, re-writing (or in even more extreme cases writing for the first time!). The purpose of monitoring and evaluation is that they should *lead* to something, they are not exercises carried out in a vacuum or simply done for their own sakes. It may be that the end product is a verification that everything is basically sound and we should simply carry on as before with all the good practices we experience every day. More likely, however, is that something will need modification or a complete 'make-over'! SENCOs need, therefore, to establish the 'parameters of power' referred to in Chapter 2 (see page 25) because action may be needed at a higher level which affects daily practice, and you need to know how far you can go. Additionally, the process of monitoring may involve classroom observations carried out by the SENCO, often involving the teaching of more senior colleagues, and again the *extent* of this and its implications for feedback and possible change need clarification and agreement.

Don't just turn up in someone else's classroom without prior discussion and agreement.

The second step is to ensure that the SENCO is comfortable with the policy itself. In many schools the SEN policy is the closest the SENCO will ever get to a job description, and even where there is a proper job description, 'implementing the school policy' is likely to be the first item. Newly appointed SENCOs rarely have the luxury of being 'in' on the initial writing of the policy! (See also Chapter 4: 'Policy formulation and implementation' page 51.) Ask these questions about the school's SEN policy to assess its compatibility with your own thinking:

- is it simply a re-hash of the main features of the Code of Practice just so we can say statutory requirements have been met?

- are there any externally driven features, such as the need to comply with the approach of an LEA to, for example, modifying the five stage descriptors?

- does the policy 'have regard to' the spirit and intentions of the Code of Practice?

- do you fully agree with any practices described or implied by the policy for such aspects as how pupils are grouped, whether pupils are withdrawn from lessons, the autonomy of a special unit, teaching strategies, advice on differentiation or gifted and talented pupils, and the use of particular diagnostic tests, programmes or resources?

- is the policy a clear statement of the underlying principles and values which describe the uniqueness of the school and its approach to special educational needs?

- is it a bland and 'woolly' document which bears no resemblance to practical reality or is it a really useful guide to how things should be done?

- is there a 'central assumption' with which you are fully in tune or against which you find yourself at odds?

You need to be ready for the inevitable *inspector's* questions:

> *Who wrote the policy? How up-to-date is it? How far do you agree with its contents? Is it fully understood by all teachers? How do you monitor its application to daily practices? How do you know that the policy works?*

and in order to do this you need a personal view on the policy itself.

The third stage is to analyse the policy for its effects on daily practice. Good policies do not go into great detail about what to do if Mary needs to take Ritalin on a Tuesday afternoon, these are *interpretative procedures* which are found in an entirely separate document (frequently updated by the SENCO and/or pastoral staff). For example, consider this aim, taken from a primary school SEN policy:

> *'To create a classroom environment which is supportive and sympathetic.'*

What does this actually *mean* for teachers, each day, in their dealings with all pupils and especially those with special needs? What are the practical implications for how pupils are grouped; which resources are used; what are the expectations of attitude and behaviour? What practical steps need to be taken to *create* this environment? What effect does this special environment have and how do we recognise the classroom which has it and the one which does not?

There are many other similar statements in policies which, quite properly, emphasise a particular set of values but which still need analysing for practical application. As a newly appointed or aspirant SENCO you cannot possibly unpick the entire policy in this way, but it will be interesting and rewarding to focus on two or three such statements because *you* are responsible for ensuring they come to pass, and for monitoring them.

Monitoring is a matter of carefully planned, often low-key, detective work. Two principles are essential:

- look at the widest possible range of evidence – it is not good practice to come to conclusions based on hearsay;
- make sure everyone involved in a monitoring process is consulted and informed beforehand about the focus and the reason for it.

Inspectors will need SENCOs to explain how they monitor the implementation of the policy. The following table lists the most commonly used methods. See how many you currently employ or plan to use in the near future.

TABLE 7.9 Monitoring methods

- Assessment data and records of pupils' achievements
- Pupils' work in several subjects
- Discussions with pupils about their work
- Discussions with parents
- Discussions with teacher colleagues
- Formal case conferences about particular pupils
- 'Tracking' individuals or groups across the curriculum
- Looking at subject/department documentation
- Looking at lesson planning and use of IEPs
- Discussions with classroom or learning assistants
- Observing teaching

Once we are satisfied that there is a workable policy, the final stage is to evaluate its effectiveness. Inspectors will expect some evaluation to have taken place so that governors can complete their report, but the newly appointed SENCO may not have been in post long enough for a thoroughly detailed evaluation.

Inspectors will not blame you if that is the case, but in terms of preparing for an inspection which may be some way off, bear these principles in mind:

- the focus for the evaluation is the effectiveness of the policy;
- there is a difference between efficiency and effectiveness:
  - *efficiency* means doing things in the right way
  - *effectiveness* means doing the right things;
- evaluation means judging the extent to which things *work*.

Evaluating an entire policy is a long-term project and one which is probably never finished. The best practice, and one which inspectors will most want to see, involves establishing a clear link between the intentions of the policy and the achievements of pupils. For example, the policy may claim that the aim of the school is to have a rigorous intervention programme for all pupils identified as being on Stage 1. Does this work? What proportion passes on to Stage 2? Is this greater/smaller than expected or about right? If smaller, does this imply a lack of resources elsewhere or is the school to be congratulated for its policy of strong early identification and intervention? If greater, are the interventions of the wrong sort?

The point needs no further elaboration. The progress pupils make is the issue and the judgement is the extent to which the policy is directly responsible for good or poor progress. Try to focus on particular gains, like improvements to reading scores or better than expected results in assessments, and track this back to a policy statement. Finally, apply this test. Think of other school policies like those on bullying or homework. These policies are designed to achieve something better in the life of the school. What is the SEN policy designed to achieve other than an understanding of the SENCO's job?

Managing the aftermath

The immediate aftermath of an inspection is a mixture of elation that it's all over, anti-climax after the emotional stress and sheer hard work, and relief at finding things were not so bad after all. Of course, if the school is judged to need special measures or to have serious weaknesses or to be underachieving, there is the added trauma of absorbing some harsh messages. As managers, SENCOs can prepare to manage the aftermath in the same way as they prepare for the inspection itself. You will find this guidance, based on the opinions of experienced SENCOs, a useful model for how to act and react.

■ Treat the inspection as a 'free' consultancy, an opportunity to gain an objective view of what you do from someone who has neither a vested interest nor an axe to grind.

■ Listen carefully to all feedback information from lessons or other activities. Have a notebook or paper with you at all times with pages or columns headed 'strengths' and 'weaknesses' and note down what is said. You can either arrange this information later or sub-divide your notes into such sections as 'teaching', 'support', 'resources', 'assessment', 'management', and note the strengths and weaknesses of each aspect.

■ Remember that the purpose of an inspection is to help the school move forward, so the 'weaknesses' are not really criticisms, they are points for future development.

■ You will be given a formal feedback on the quality of SEN provision, the standards and progress of pupils, the effectiveness of teaching and learning support, and the efficiency of procedures. Listen to this carefully but do not let your mind dwell on any one point or you will miss the next one. Take notes if there is nobody else with you to do so, but it is always a good idea to have senior management representation to reinforce the notion of SEN as a whole school issue.

■ The formal feedback to you will consist of 'headline judgements' and the inspector may still not have all the detailed comments from colleagues. Yet all subjects will be given their own detailed feedback on the progress made by pupils with SEN, so find the time to talk to all heads of department or subject coordinators about what was said to them about special needs. Record these comments on your 'strengths and weaknesses' sheets.

■ Do not rely too much on the final written report. Special needs will rate a sentence or two in most sections or there may be longer statements about particular strengths or weaknesses. In any case it will be at least six weeks after the inspection before the report appears, and that six weeks represents an important time for SENCOs to build up the broadest possible picture from all sources.

■ Gather as much information as you can during each day of an inspection: meet with support staff and ask them what was 'seen' and if any comment about their work was made.

- Conduct your own feedback. As a manager you will be at least partly responsible for what others do and colleagues will be anxious to know the balance of strengths and weaknesses. Remember, no scapegoating! You are all in it together and must share the criticisms as well as the plaudits.

- When you feel that you have the broadest possible picture based on inspectors' judgements, take time for reflection: is this a true and accurate picture of the state of special needs in your school? Assuming that there are no major disagreements and that you view the inspectors' judgements to be accurate and soundly based, draw up a short summary of the main points for development with some suggestions for methods of implementation and present this to senior management. This has two effects: first, it shows how deeply you are thinking about future development and second, it indicates a desire to move forward along proper management lines by not absolving senior management of all responsibility. Too many SENCOs take inspections personally and work in isolation to tackle weaknesses.

- Do not rush to change things immediately. Many SENCOs make the mistake of thinking that they must start doing things differently straightaway. This is a recipe for making the wrong decisions. Remember the old adage: act in haste, repent at leisure. Ponder the priorities, discuss with colleagues, focus on just one or two major issues for now and draw up an action plan.

- A good action plan demonstrates ten clear principles:
  - complete understanding of the issue;
  - appreciation of what is realistically possible;
  - wider implications for the work of others;
  - clear vision of the principal objective;
  - a stepped series of unambiguous actions;
  - clear responsibilities, timescales and costs if appropriate;
  - agreed 'milestones' or review points;
  - the involvement of more than one person;
  - a mixture of discrete and interlocking tasks;
  - a clearly stated definite end point.

Table 7.10 gives a model template for an action plan based on the aftermath of an inspection. This table concludes this final section of the chapter.

TABLE 7.10 Action plan template

Actions needed following inspection

ISSUE					ANTICIPATED ISSUE RESOLUTION TIMESCALE .... MONTHS
PRECISE POINT(S) RAISED BY INSPECTORS					
OBJECTIVE FOR ACTION					
ACTIONS OR TASKS	BY WHOM	BY WHEN NEEDED	METHOD	RESOURCES	REVIEW DATE ✓ WHEN COMPLETED

ANNEX 1 New Inspection Framework

The new Inspection Framework, in operation from January 2000, contains an inspection schedule presented in the form of a series of questions which inspectors must answer and which the format of the report on the school must reflect. Special Educational Needs must be covered in the answers to all questions. SENCOs should use the questions to assist them in school self-evaluation.

The Inspection Schedule

1 What sort of school is it?

2 How high are the standards?

> **2.1** The school's results and achievements

> **2.2** Pupils' attitudes, values and personal development

3 How well are the pupils taught?

4 How good are the curricular and other opportunities offered to pupils?

5 How well does the school care for its pupils?

6 How well does the school work in partnership with parents?

7 How well is the school led and managed?

8 What should the school do to improve further?

9 What is the quality of other specified features? (e.g. SEN unit)

10 What are the standards and what is the quality of teaching in areas of the curriculum, subjects and courses?

ANNEX 2 'Short' inspections

The new Inspection Framework, in operation from January 2000, introduced the concept of 'short' inspections for schools judged to be successful or improving significantly. These inspections are designed to meet the minimum requirements of section 10 of the School Inspection Act 1996 by reporting on:

- the quality of education provided by the school;

- the educational standards achieved in the school;

- whether the financial resources made available to the school are managed efficiently; and

- the spiritual, moral, social and cultural development of pupils at the school.

This type of inspection is called *short* because:

- it is carried out by a small team of inspectors, ranging from two in the smallest primary to five in the largest secondary school;

- the duration of the inspection will range from one day to three days according to the size of the school, but will rarely be more than three days long.

Short inspections differ from *full* inspections in that:

- they do not report specifically and separately on the standards and the quality of teaching in each subject, course or curriculum area;

- each key question of the inspection schedule is not evaluated in the same depth and detail as for *full* inspections;

- there is less pressure and workload on teachers because the number of observed lessons is considerably reduced and not every teacher is seen teaching;

- teachers will not be given a summative profile of their teaching at the end of the inspection;

- there will be no formal feedback on the strengths and weaknesses of each subject;

- schools will be able to negotiate specific areas of focus with inspectors; and

- the final report will be a commentary based on an evaluation of what the school does well and what could be improved.

Full inspections are led by subjects and aspects of the school, *short* inspections are led by issues. One such 'issue' may well be SEN, and inspectors need to 'get to the heart' of what makes provision in the school so different from others. There will therefore be a more rigorous pursuit of evidence by more than one inspector and more sampling of the work of pupils as they reach the end of a key stage. Standards, teaching and management will be the focus, and of particular relevance to SENCOs will be the attention paid to how the school monitors and evaluates its own work. Because time is limited, documentation, records and paperwork must be spot on and SENCOs should be prepared to direct inspectors towards lessons of particular interest. Samples of work done by pupils with SEN should be readily available and SENCOs should expect to be questioned closely about how SEN provision is coordinated across the whole curriculum. In essence, be on top of the job!

———— Summary ————

- Inspectors see all aspects of how a school performs as interrelated issues. Each whole school issue entails whole school management and the judgements on special needs are made in the context of a whole school approach.

- Central to the work of SENCOs is the coordination of provision for special needs across the whole curriculum, so considerable emphasis should be placed on knowledge of the curriculum and encouraging an approach to fitting the curriculum to the child rather than the other way round.

- In assessing pupils' needs SENCOs need to use the widest possible range of sources of information and it is the responsibility of SENCOs to coordinate how that information is collected.

- Inspectors will focus on how pupils' needs are identified, what provision is supplied to meet those needs and what the outcome then is as expressed as pupils' achievements. These aspects are investigated through seven key judgements and SENCOs should be able to supply evidence for each of them.

- Some of the evidence is expressed in the form of school documentation. SENCOs can influence the contents and quality of school documents, the most important of which are subject development plans and the whole school policy for special needs.

- Governors should publish an evaluation of the effectiveness of the policy and SENCOs should demonstrate how such evaluations are made.

- Other documents may contain valuable management information so these should be highlighted.

- Inspectors judge management by its effects. Professional knowledge and management expertise can be demonstrated by the way special needs permeates whole school thinking and planning.

- The most powerful demonstration is where teachers know what they are doing and why, and where policies and practices are seen to be consistently applied.

- SENCOs should ensure that there is a clear link between their management decisions and improvements to the quality of teaching and learning.

- The OFSTED judgements on standards and progress will reveal much about how special needs are managed in the school and there are several specific tasks which SENCOs can undertake to boost overall standards.

- Where there are notable examples of successes these should be highlighted, with convincing explanations.

- Inspectors must judge the extent of the school's compliance with statutory requirements. The most important of these relates to 'having regard to' the Code of Practice and following the regulations governing statutory assessments and statements.

- Policy evaluation is also a statutory requirement so SENCOs should develop straightforward systems for monitoring aspects of the school policy so that judgements about its effectiveness can be made.

- Immediately following an inspection it is important to absorb the messages about the strengths and weaknesses of the school's approach to special needs.

- SENCOs should draw up an action plan but should not work alone on this, there should be a whole school response to developmental issues.

Tailpiece

Progress, according to George Bernard Shaw, is a product of being unreasonable. Writing in 1903 in 'Man and Superman' he argued:

> *'The reasonable man adapts himself to the world; the unreasonable one persists in trying to adapt the world to himself. Therefore all progress depends on the unreasonable man.'*

Of course, this is not to say that all SENCOs should make themselves unreasonable if they are to make progress in the post, but Shaw's remark does point us in the right direction. First, it illustrates the fact that the SENCO role is continually evolving because experienced practitioners have refused to accept things as they are and constantly seek to change the culture within which SEN operates in schools. Second, it nicely sums up the attitude SENCOs should have towards the need for the curriculum to be adapted to the child and not the other way round. Finally, it highlights the need for persistence as a means of accomplishing goals.

Moving forward in the role

As a newly appointed SENCO you will be aware of the scores of tasks, some small and some daunting, which make up the post. You will be aware, too, of how the school expects things to be done for the good of the children within it. This book has focused on some of the most significant responsibilities and outlined the management perspective. As was said at the beginning, this is not a book about teaching children with special educational needs, that is for other publications. However, this is the single most important aspect of the job so time must be devoted to it. The aim of this book so far has been to demonstrate how management efficiency can create more time. Conclusions are apt to summarise and present overviews, but this is not the intention here. The assumption behind this Tailpiece is that novice SENCOs wish to take the role forward successfully and refine their management skills still further. The book will have filled in some gaps in knowledge and expertise, but others remain, and I hope that you will have taken full advantage of the action plan at the end of Chapter 2 to note aspects for future development.

By looking back at the ten key questions raised in 'How to use this book', this final section gives guidance on broad areas for further exploration such as managing change and a holistic approach to curriculum coordination. Bearing in mind that management is about *people* and all the rest is administration, there is a further examination of the SENCO's mentoring and advisory role. The Tailpiece ends with a short explanation of the role of managers in quality control and quality assurance.

The sub-title of this book is 'Maximising your potential'. *Potential* implies an innate ability which has yet to show itself fully, but it also implies a willingness to learn and practise new skills which will not necessarily have an immediate impact. As more schools take the view that provision for special educational needs is neither export (something which takes place beyond the boundaries of the 'normal' curriculum) nor import (specialist teachers brought into the classroom) but an internalised process common to all teachers, it is clear that the SENCO role has developed into one of advocating and facilitating change in teaching and learning. The duties expounded by the Code of Practice must, of course, be carried out, but many SENCOs wish to go beyond this and develop their expertise in research, staff training or management. Some expert practitioners are well down the road of developing all three and this must be the ultimate goal of teachers new to the post.

———— Returning to the ten questions ————

The ten questions which appear on page xxiv were distilled from four newly appointed SENCOs' responses to a questionnaire. Amongst other technical questions was the request to list the most pressing issues about the administrative and management roles *as they saw them*, immediately after assuming the post. Seven chapters later, let us revisit those questions, but not necessarily in the order in which they appear because they can be linked thematically.

1   What will be my main responsibilities and to whom am I accountable for their discharge?

The main responsibilities still remain those listed by the Code of Practice but can be reduced to two main functional duties: oversight of the school's SEN policy and coordinating provision across the curriculum. The question of accountability is more complex. In broad terms it was the widespread failure of the teaching profession to accept that it was accountable for the quality of the 'product' in return for the investment of vast sums of public money which led to the major reforms of the 1980s. Much has been written about models of accountability as a result of this change to the dominant culture of policy making. What all these models have in common is the assertion that patterns of accountability in schools are determined by the overarching ideology of the institution, which usually means that of the headteacher. For example, 'bureaucratic' accountability is characterised by job descriptions, adherence to contracts of employment and a hierarchical management structure dominated by the task of assessing the competence of individuals in fulfilling contractual obligations. Accountability is thus defined in terms of position in the hierarchy. 'Professional' accountability views the teacher as an autonomous expert within a culture of dialogue and school self-evaluation. Teachers see their responsibility as being to a wide variety of 'clients', especially pupils and their parents, and there is a culture of collegiality in decision making. In this model accountability is defined in terms of professional relationships and processes which may vary according to the methods the school chooses to address its priorities. The 'partnership' model extends the principles of the professional approach still further by lending equal weight to the views of parents as the consumers and to teachers as the providers. Early pioneers of 'home/school agreements' were thus paving the way for a partnership model. This model depends upon shared objectives and the concept of competing with other schools via 'open enrolment'. Within all schools, then, is a complex web of accountability to oneself and professional colleagues, to pupils and parents, to the school's leadership structure and to society at large through such aspects as performance indicators.

For new SENCOs seeking to develop the role this brings us back to the relationship with the headteacher and the school's expectations of the role in action, especially with regard to the spending of money. It is precisely because obtaining and allocating financial resources to special educational needs, with the guarantee of value for money, has become so central to the management of SEN that so many headteachers have taken on the SENCO role for themselves. Where a separate SENCO is employed everything depends on the degree to which management responsibility is delegated. In simple terms these two models are observed in schools:

Minor delegation = SENCO as administrator + full teaching load

Major delegation = SENCO as middle manager + reduced teaching load

and it is very difficult for the recipient of minor delegation to take the role forward other than by refining the administrative systems. However, for those SENCOs in a more favoured position, 'accountability' can begin to be measured in financial terms and, therefore, so can the capacity for the role development. SENCOs need to develop an understanding of the costs involved in effective provision because 'creating the conditions for success' – an essential function of management – ultimately depends upon how resources are obtained and deployed. This involves a careful analysis of the exact nature of school needs and knowledge of the source and extent of funding. Many SENCOs see the extent of their financial involvement as the benchmark by which to judge the degree of management responsibility delegated to them.

The essential point of *development* here is in the role of the SENCO as an advocate. Only the well informed SENCO can argue a balanced case for additional funding or take the decision to deploy LSAs in different ways.

TASK 42

Accountability and developing advocacy

Which model of accountability best fits your current situation?

Meet with your school's key curriculum managers to discuss ways in which the whole school can become more accountable for SEN. Agree common objectives.

Discuss with the headteacher the way in which you can become more involved with the financing of SEN.

Investigate the unit cost per pupil of the current level of provision for SEN. Argue the case for the employment of one more LSA on the basis of what percentage increase in unit costs this would generate.

2   How has the SENCO role developed since its inception and how can I influence further development?
5   How can I learn, develop and practise new management skills
AND
9   How do I become an effective team leader?

Much of this book has demonstrated the ways in which the SENCO role has expanded beyond the definition in the Code of Practice. The essence of the shift has been away from working with pupils towards working with teachers. As management is about working with people to achieve common objectives, this represents a management shift as well. Further development of the SENCO's role must therefore be seen as management development. The four areas which new SENCOs should consider in advancing their management skills are style, motivation, training and research.

Management style is a product of individual personality, the numbers of colleagues to be 'managed' and the organisational structure of the school. Chapter 5, for example, shows how policy making can be influenced by either a 'political' or 'collegiate' structure and we have just seen how the concept of accountability is affected by prevailing ideologies. Research into management styles in all types of institutions, including schools, suggests that the most common problem is in reconciling the demands of the organisation and the needs of the individual. The danger in many schools today is that the concept of the teacher as the autonomous professional is being sidelined by the pressure to perform against measurable indicators. In adopting a particular 'style' of management SENCOs must acknowledge that colleagues will perform better if their attitudes and opinions are understood and valued.

There is an extensive canon of literature about management styles, all of which ultimately points us in the same direction. At one extreme is the view that the only function of management is to clarify goals and at the other is the concept of 'managerless management' of the sort tried, and quickly abandoned, by the army of the People's Republic of China, which abolished the concept of 'rank'. Most theories, such as those of Peter Drucker and Douglas McGregor, take as their basis the concept of a manager being concerned with tasks and people. The task-orientated manager will have low concern for people, whereas the people-orientated manager will have low concern for the task. As managers develop their skills they move to a point where concern for both is roughly equal and then progress beyond that to what many believe to be the 'ideal' state: *team* or *democratic* management where both the people and the task are held in equally high regard. This also equates to what is frequently referred to as *participative* management in which goals are set and procedures are agreed only after incorporating the opinions and suggestions of the group. In this style performance indicators exist as tools of self evaluation rather than control systems. For SENCOs the development of management style therefore becomes a process of moving towards participation and away from an over-emphasis on either tasks or people.

The question of management style naturally influences the motivation of those who are being managed. One good way for SENCOs to take their managerial role forward is to focus on how to motivate colleagues not only to 'perform' better but also to develop their knowledge and expertise to new levels. Studies of motivational factors in schools show that teachers attach great value to achievement, recognition and responsibility. Bearing these three in mind, a greater degree of participation in the management of SEN should improve motivation. This develops through a process of 'opening up' to others the four classic management tasks: *defining* the objectives, *planning* the strategy, *briefing* the participants and *monitoring* the outcomes. How much of this do you currently entrust to others?

The SENCO's role in training others is pivotal to the success of SEN provision in any school. Most SENCOs are called upon to advise colleagues on the development of resources or the use of particular teaching methods, and leading group discussions during training days is very common. How, then, can SENCOs develop this further in ways which promote teamwork and a collegiate approach to problem-solving? One way is to adopt a method known as *reflective practice*. This is a particular staged system and is not the same as allowing teachers time to reflect upon their own needs. Reflective practice is a process of systematically analysing how theories can inform practice. Originally based on the work of D Kolb (1984), the system depends upon a cycle in which a problem arises in some tangible form; this leads to the collection of precise data about the problem and an analysis of this information; the problem is then removed from its 'real' context and re-expressed in theoretical terms so that theoretical solutions can be explored without practical constraints; the theoretical solutions are applied to the practical problem and evaluated for effectiveness; and the problem is either solved or redefined. SENCOs who have used this method in staff development exercises have found that it leads to innovative and creative, therefore motivating, approaches to problem solving. One SENCO found, for example, that the 'problems' associated with teaching a particular group were nothing to do with the group or the teaching.

This approach to staff development is also an example of how SENCOs can take the role forward in terms of *action research*. One certain way of encouraging participation, especially by LSAs, is to develop a research project. This focuses on the individual and the team as reflective learners and could take many forms. For example, research into teaching methods to help dyslectic pupils could assist the SENCO in coordinating curriculum provision for these children. Alternatively, the requirement for governors to comment on the effectiveness of the school's policy generates a major annual research and evaluation project.

3 How do I prepare the whole school for the challenges of inclusive education?
AND
4 How can I influence the curriculum and teacher colleagues especially when SEN pupils cannot meet school or national targets?
AND
7 How can I ensure that children make good progress in all curriculum areas?

These three questions are combined because the common theme is curriculum management and this is a topic which permeates the whole book. Managing provision across the whole curriculum involves so many of the planning, policy making and target-setting processes described in different chapters and brought together in the individual topics of Chapter 5.

One way of taking this forward is to adopt a *whole child/whole curriculum* approach to proactive curriculum management. Given that coordinating curriculum provision is the SENCO's central activity and that this takes on a challenging dimension if we subscribe to current inclusion theories which place the curriculum rather than the child at the heart of the SEN issue, it follows that the way the curriculum is managed says much about the extension of management skills. 'Moving the role forward' means moving forward the four pillars of management referred to earlier: defining, planning, briefing and monitoring.

Defining means bringing together a task group to establish a definition of the curriculum. This creates the opportunity to form a group on the basis of interest, influence and team member 'type' rather than imposing an additional task on an existing group. It also provides a chance for LSAs and other professional support staff to have a focus outside working with individual pupils. In management terms this leads to the development and practice of leadership skills (doing the right things), entails negotiation with senior management on the authority and terms of reference of the group, and models the participative style. In curriculum terms what we are aiming at is not a redefinition of the whole curriculum, *it is a new definition of the SEN curriculum*. Secondary schools have further to travel in this regard than primary schools. Primary schools have always emphasised the requirement to teach children, secondary schools have stressed the importance of teaching subjects, and the management structures of the two sets of institutions reflect this dichotomy. The task is to create a 'skills rich' curriculum based on a list of essential generic skills which both open up access to all subjects and at the same time can be taught or reinforced by all subjects within the existing National Curriculum framework. Many schools have used this approach to create policies for literacy or numeracy across the curriculum, but this time the focus is upon the needs of particular segments of the school population. The promotion of generic skills in each curriculum area can therefore be an objective focus for development planning at both subject and whole school level and can inform the staff development programme.

Planning not only involves synthesising subject perspectives, it offers the opportunity for SENCOs to practise defining and clarifying goals in response to the wide range of needs displayed by pupils. It also implies planning for change and action research into the ways children learn. Planning for change is a complex process about which much has been written. However, change must not be seen as an end in itself and somehow divorced from the 'normal' practices of good management already elaborated upon in this book. Change will be effective only if it is accompanied by shared and clear objectives, if the desired change is seen to be 'worthwhile' in terms of improvements to teaching and learning, and it is tackled in a spirit of collaboration and team participation.

Figure 8.1 offers a process model for managing change. This model identifies and describes the key stages in the change management cycle and emphasises, yet again, the need for everyone to be very clear about the intended outcome. In this instance we are aiming for a skills-based definition of the SEN curriculum which will direct the thinking behind IEPs, development planning, policy making, target setting and the monitoring of pupils' achievements. Above all, it will provide a sense of purpose to the SENCO's role of coordinating curriculum provision by moving away from a literacy-based view of special educational needs towards a broader skills base.

FIG. 8.1 Process model for managing change

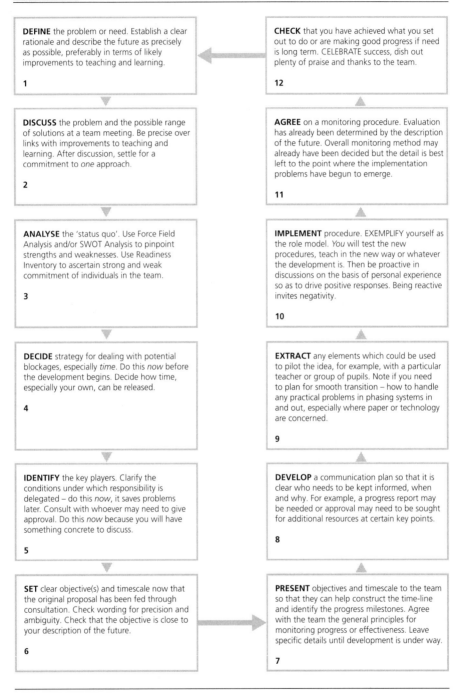

DEFINE the problem or need. Establish a clear rationale and describe the future as precisely as possible, preferably in terms of likely improvements to teaching and learning.

1

DISCUSS the problem and the possible range of solutions at a team meeting. Be precise over links with improvements to teaching and learning. After discussion, settle for a commitment to *one* approach.

2

ANALYSE the 'status quo'. Use Force Field Analysis and/or SWOT Analysis to pinpoint strengths and weaknesses. Use Readiness Inventory to ascertain strong and weak commitment of individuals in the team.

3

DECIDE strategy for dealing with potential blockages, especially *time*. Do this *now* before the development begins. Decide how time, especially your own, can be released.

4

IDENTIFY the key players. Clarify the conditions under which responsibility is delegated – do this *now*, it saves problems later. Consult with whoever may need to give approval. Do this *now* because you will have something concrete to discuss.

5

SET clear objective(s) and timescale now that the original proposal has been fed through consultation. Check wording for precision and ambiguity. Check that the objective is close to your description of the future.

6

CHECK that you have achieved what you set out to do or are making good progress if need is long term. CELEBRATE success, dish out plenty of praise and thanks to the team.

12

AGREE on a monitoring procedure. Evaluation has already been determined by the description of the future. Overall monitoring method may already have been decided but the detail is best left to the point where the implementation problems have begun to emerge.

11

IMPLEMENT procedure. EXEMPLIFY yourself as the role model. *You* will test the new procedures, teach in the new way or whatever the development is. Then be proactive in discussions on the basis of personal experience so as to drive positive responses. Being reactive invites negativity.

10

EXTRACT any elements which could be used to pilot the idea, for example, with a particular teacher or group of pupils. Note if you need to plan for smooth transition – how to handle any practical problems in phasing systems in and out, especially where paper or technology are concerned.

9

DEVELOP a communication plan so that it is clear who needs to be kept informed, when and why. For example, a progress report may be needed or approval may need to be sought for additional resources at certain key points.

8

PRESENT objectives and timescale to the team so that they can help construct the time-line and identify the progress milestones. Agree with the team general principles for monitoring progress or effectiveness. Leave specific details until development is under way.

7

Any curriculum development has to be seen as a process which will enhance learning and it is especially important for SENCOs as the leaders of curriculum change to be knowledgeable about the process of learning itself. There are almost as many theories about learning as there are children in our schools. The two polarities of learning theory may also be seen as opposing armies on a political battleground with the prize to the victorious being the National Curriculum itself:

'Traditional model'	Versus	'Progressive model'
Passive reception of knowledge, teacher is responsible for imparting knowledge in a formal style, learning is linear and sequential		Learning is based on discovery, the learner is active and eager, the style is informal and teachers are seen as 'facilitators'.

In using this example of managing curriculum development to move the role forward, SENCOs should take as much time as possible over this planning stage. For example, seeing management as a series of interlocking processes would prompt a *reflective practice* approach to planning which in turn would spawn an action research project into the theories of learning. In this instance the brief could be to produce a 'deficit model' of learning in relation to SEN by taking the current view that learners learn by being shown new knowledge which they then have to interpret through their existing knowledge. The challenge for a curriculum for SEN is a return to the 'gap theory' of Chapter 5: making sure the distance between new and existing knowledge is not too wide for children to cross without clearly marked stepping stones. As pointers, the research team could look at the work of that good friend of teacher training colleges everywhere, Piaget, and move on to consider Vygotsky's theories and the more recent work on multiple intelligences by Howard Gardner. Having curriculum change linked to changes in learning patterns supported by theoretical research is a good foundation for planning.

Briefing for this form of curriculum structure offers the SENCO opportunities to develop and practise a number of skills, and in particular:

- *chairing meetings*   –   keeping the focus on the objectives and promoting collaboration;
- *one-to-one mentoring*   –   working with teachers to develop an approach to skills teaching based on adaptations to the content of subject schemes of work;

- *cascade*   – working through subject coordinators in a process of non-threatening professional dialogue which acknowledges their own responsibilities; and

- *presentations*   – preparing a discussion paper and taking the whole staff through it with a recommended and well reasoned action plan.

The aim of briefing is 'to get everyone on board' in a way that enhances their perceptions of teaching rather than hampers them. The focus is therefore on positive outcomes and clear objectives.

Monitoring is the final stage in using this aspect of curriculum development to take the SENCO forward. Good use should be made of the guidance already given in this book on monitoring in relation to policy making and development planning. The opportunity here is to involve other people (like LSAs) in not only carrying out the monitoring but in devising the methods. This is what is commonly known as 'transition management' and it involves working backwards from the ideal future state as defined in the objectives for change to pinpoint the 'milestones' along the way. Monitoring is thus a process of measuring progress against agreed criteria rather than the arbitrary use of the word 'termly' which is commonly found in development plans. Monitoring will focus on the outcomes of the change rather than the timescale.

TASK 43

Monitoring

Imagine that you are planning the introduction of a skills-defined SEN curriculum. Set out the desired outcome as a series of sequentially related goals, but without timescales.

Identify the means by which the accomplishment of these goals can be observed or measured. Do not mention time.

6   How do I combine whole school responsibilities with a significant personal teaching commitment?

To a large degree this is the underpinning theme of this book. All teachers occupying some form of middle management role in schools see this as a central issue, especially in primary schools where there is not the generosity of non-contact time enjoyed by secondary colleagues. The first step is to adopt the positive view that if you accept the additional post of responsibility you also accept the need to manage time effectively. There are books on time management and there are courses on time management but what they all have in common is a misnomer for a title. Time is only abstract to astro-physicists and it is only elastic to small children at bedtime! Time cannot be managed, but what goes into it can.

In terms of moving the role forward there are no magic secrets to this. This book shows how a more efficient and effective response to the many responsibilities of a SENCO's role helps to reduce the amount of time needed to be spent on them. However, there are two ways in which SENCOs can create more space for developmental work: delegation and the use of supply cover to reduce teaching commitments. The latter is a contentious issue and depends largely on familiarity, trust and confidence. Suffice it to say that 'intelligent' schools use temporary teachers in intelligent ways and budget properly for developmental work. Effective delegation should be the principal aim of SENCOs who wish to move the role forward and this really is a long-term project. It also illustrates perfectly the interlocking nature of the responsibilities because only by concentrating on the *advisory* role will SENCOs create a feeling of confidence in the colleagues to whom tasks or responsibilities are delegated, thus creating both the participatory style needed for successful management and the time for development.

8   How do I influence the construction of a school policy for SEN which places and maintains SEN at the centre of school life and not on the margin?

Like the Code of Practice, this book advocates the view that SEN is a whole school issue. The whole question of policy formulation is covered specifically in Chapter 4 and theoretical issues are explored in relation to 'giftedness' in Chapter 5. Keeping this topic moving forward is to a large extent dependent on the process of evaluating and reporting on the effectiveness of the policy annually by the governing body. The way the SENCO and the rest of the team view the evaluative role in terms of establishing the monitoring criteria will largely determine whether the policy is an active or dormant document. Keeping and developing the whole school focus can be achieved in a combination of four ways.

■ Encouraging a 'culture of enquiry' amongst colleagues. All schools should be developing this anyway as they seek to improve their overall effectiveness as places of learning. Teachers should be challenged by the SENCO to examine their methods, try new resources and create situations in their classrooms which reinforce success rather than emphasise failure. This shifts the balance in favour of a 'can do' approach to teaching children with special educational needs.

■ Linked to this culture and a way of obtaining it is for SENCOs to move their advisory and mentoring role up a gear towards the creation of special interest or 'focus' groups. This can be achieved in any school, whatever the size or type, because there is no lower limit to the size of the group. The idea is to change the core activity away from 'what to do about Johnny' to 'how to tackle autism' or any one of a number of such topics. There is then a greater credibility to the advice and a greater willingness to take risks in teaching because the strategy is a group one.

■ By constantly seeking to sharpen the focus of development planning both at subject and whole school level, SENCOs can give real purpose to the policy. To move forward SENCOs need to analyse the SEN content of previous plans and evaluate the success or otherwise of the objectives. This will give a clearer picture of specific training needs and enable the SENCO to present a training plan to senior management. The development and delivery of a training plan is a good example of a forward-looking project.

■ Using the requirement to employ IEPs and the fact that teachers are now comfortable with the concept, SENCOs can develop the subject content more consistently away from purely literacy-based targets. Allied to this is using the same planning techniques to produce Pastoral Support Plans and Individual Behaviour Plans. This helps to broaden the notion of support for pupils across different aspects of school life.

TASK 44

Identifying the management role

Analyse each of the four suggestions above into concrete practical tasks under the headings: *defining; planning; briefing; monitoring.*

10   How do I cope with an OFSTED inspection?

This question has been thoroughly answered in Chapter 7. There is only one way in which this topic can be taken forward for the benefit of SENCOs who wish to develop their role and that is by examining the issue of *quality*. The concept of Total Quality Management (TQM) is beginning to have an impact on schools and is an aspect of industrial or business management which figures prominently in headteacher training courses. Aspects are filtering down to other levels of school management through common expressions such as Quality Control and Quality Assurance. Some simple definitions will help to clarify the issue under consideration:

- *Quality control* is concerned with checking that some product or service is of a suitable standard of excellence *after it has been provided*; whereas

- *Quality assurance* is concerned with the steps taken by the workforce themselves *internally as the work progresses* to make sure that the product or service is of the highest possible standard in the first place.

  In educational terms a contrast can therefore be made between the OFSTED inspector who visits schools to inspect the quality of teaching and learning using external criteria, and to hold teachers accountable for meeting those criteria after a number of years – *quality control*; and internal self-evaluation by the teachers themselves using internal criteria as they go along, together with development activity so that they always provide the best teaching and learning possible – *quality assurance*.

- *Total Quality Management* is therefore the process by which a school adds the quality dimension to its list of monitoring and evaluation procedures. It is how quality assurance operates in action and becomes added to the top of the list of school aims.

As time goes by more and more OFSTED inspections will focus not on the quality of what schools do *but on how they monitor their own quality* and what they do with the conclusions reached. This points the way forward for SENCOs who wish to develop their role further, and it is fitting that we should conclude on the 'quality' issue. Before moving on to new developments SENCOs should take a critical look at what happens *now* from the point of view of *quality* and ask:

'Is the provision for special educational needs in this school the very best that we can possibly achieve?' 'In what areas are we deficient and lacking knowledge and resources?' 'Are pupils being failed by the system in our school?' *Why?*

References

Adair, J (1983)	*Effective Leadership*	London: Pan
Baldridge, J V et al (1978)	*Policy Making and Effective Leadership*	San Francisco: Jossey Bass
Belbin, M (1981)	*Management Teams: Why they Succeed or Fail*	London: Heinemann
Bennett, N (1995)	*Managing Professional Teachers*	London: Paul Chapman
Crawford, M, Kydd, L and Parker, S (1994)	*Education Management in Action*	London: Paul Chapman
DFE	*Code of Practice on the Identification and Assessment of Special Educational Needs*	HMSO
DfEE	*Supporting the Target Setting Process*	London: DfEE Publications
Drucker, P (1954)	*The Practice of Management*	New York: Harper & Brothers
Everard, B and Morris, G (1990)	*Effective School Management*	London: Paul Chapman
Gardner, H (1993)	*Multiple Intelligences: The Theory in Practice*	New York: Basic Books
Hargreaves, D and Hopkins, D (1991)	*The Empowered School: The Management and Practice of Development Planning*	London: Cassell
Kolb, D (1984)	*Experiential Learning: Experience as the Source of Learning and Development*	London: Prentice Hall

MacGilchrist, B, Myers, K and Reed J (1997)	*The Intelligent School*	London: Paul Chapman
MacGilchrist, B et al (1995)	*Planning Matters*	London: Paul Chapman
McGregor, D (1960)	*The Human Side of Enterprise*	New York: McGraw-Hill
OFSTED	*Pupils with Specific Learning Difficulties in Mainstream Schools*	London: HMCI Report
OFSTED	*The SEN Code of Practice: Three Years On*	London: HMCI Report
Piaget, J (1932)	*The Language and Thought of the Child*, 2nd edition	London: Penguin
Shuttleworth, V (2000)	*Middle Management In Schools Manual*	London: Financial Times/ Prentice Hall
Smith, A (1996)	*Accelerated Learning in the Classroom Framework*	London: Educational Press
Tuckman, B W (1965)	*Psychological Bulletin*, Vol. 63	
Vygotsky, L (1987)	*The Collected Works of L. S. Vygotsky*, Vol. 1, R. Reiber and A. Carton (eds)	London: Plenum

Index